MASTER YOUR MARRIAGE

Dr Bhoopalam Sunil

RIGI PUBLICATION

All right reserved

Master Your Marriage

By

Dr Bhoopalam Sunil

Originally published in India

ISBN: 978-93-89540-76-5 (Paperback)
978-93-89540-77-2 (eBook)

Published by RIGI PUBLICATION

777, Street no.9, Krishna Nagar Khanna-141401 (Punjab), India
Website: www.rigipublication.com

Email: info@rigipublication.com

Phone: +91-9357710014, +91-9465468291

FOREWORD

If you are not totally happy or are struggling to make your marriage a happy one, this book is for you. This book is written for all those people who are finding it difficult to have a smooth run in their married life. It is not true that marriages are not easy. I would say marriages take work to run smooth and if you are willing to put in that work into your marriage, you'll be heading towards creating a beautiful life for yourself and your partner.

This book talks about various aspects that needs to be looked into in order to build a happy marriage, and in turn a happier life. This book is going to help you find answers to some of the most commonly asked questions by any person who is having a hard time getting along well with the marriage. Some of the topics include:

- How to deal with disappointments in marriage?
- How to re-build trust in your relationship?
- What makes life partners best partners?
- Why do people say 'Honesty is the best policy' especially in building a successful marriage?
- How to build emotional intimacy even after years of being married?
- How to deal with an angry spouse?

The unique feature of this book is that it is down-to-earth practical. I have focused on providing simple, usable techniques and solutions that you can easily apply in your everyday life. These solutions do not take a big chunk of your time. All they take is a willingness to make your marriage better than what it is now and if you have gathered that willingness, your war is half fought already! Dive deep in into each topic I've talked about and figure out for yourself how you can apply these into your marriage. I hope this book helps you in walking towards a happy marriage and building your very own heaven as life partners. I wish each one of you a happy read!!!

ABOUT THE AUTHOR

Dr Bhoopalam Sunil

Bhoopalam Family is a well-known family in Shimoga, Bhoopalam Chandrashekariah was a great freedom fighter.

Bhoopalam Chandrashekariah was the General Secretary of VHP. His younger brother Bhoopalam Puttananjappa was a M.A. gold medalist and a leading lawyer in late 60s. Bhoopalam Puttananjappa's elder son was Bhoopalam Mahabala who was captain of YMCA Cricket team and president of the club 'The Bangalore City Institute". He was a leading textile merchant and partner of Tallam Nanjunda Setty. Bhoopalam Mahabala's eldest son was Bhoopalam Sunil born on 18-01-1967. Bhoopalam Sunil did his schooling in Baldwins & Valleys. Bhoopalam Sunil studied in National College. He completed B.A., B.B.A. and M.B.A.

Dr Bhoopalam Sunil is a reputed author, writer and a poet. His books crackling jocks for all and commonly confused words is published by JAICO and KINNARI Publications. His articles are published in Deccan Herald, Indian Express and several magazines.

Dr Bhoopalam Sunil established Gandhi Old Age Home in 2001 There are 125 inmates, who are old people. The inmates are given free food free accommodation, free clothes, free medicines and free insurance policies. Dr Bhoopalam Sunil mobilized funds for the buildings at Gandhi Old Age Home through Rotarys., Lions, Round Table and many other charitable institutions.

There are 18 staff people to look after them. The home is around 50,000 Sq.ft. Medical Education Minister Ramachandre Gowda had inaugurated a Ganapathi temple in Gandhi Old Age Home in the year 2014. Incidentally, Dr. Bhoopalam Sunil has received many awards to date. Some of them are

- Jai Prakash Narayan National Award
- Visweshwaraian Global Award for Excellence
- Aryabhatta Award
- Rajya Ratna Award
- Adarsha Ratha Award
- Karnataka Padmashree Award
- Environment Award

- Dr. Bhoopalam Sunil received Honarary doctorate in the year 2017.
- He is the chairman of Advisory board of Kannada T.V.
- He is the Vice President of Karnataka Arya Vyshya Sahithya Parishad.
- He is the Business development chairman of world Arya Vyshya Mahasabha.
- He is the vice president of Vasavi Temple Kothnur, Banasvadi.
- He is the chairman of Vasavi Raktha Chetana Trust.
- He is the Deputy Governer of Vasavi Clubs International.
- He is the Joint Secretary of Karnataka Arya Vyshya Maha Mandali.
- Dr Bhoopalam Sunil has interviewed many social dignitaries for the magazine Environment Pollution, where he is the sub-editor.
- He has interviewed Joint Commissioner of GST Pratap Kumar and Gopinath Commissioner Income tax.

DEDICATION

I Dr Bhoopalam Sunil dedicate this book to my parents.
Bhoopalam Suvarna and B P Mahabala

Author's family

(In the photo)

Dr Bhoopalam Sunil, Prem Kumar, Baby Ritanya
Shruthika and Sunitha

Shri Sadananda Gowda central minister for chemicals and fertilizers released stamps on Gandhi Old Age Home and Dr Bhoopalam Sunil

CONTENTS

What makes a loving and an enduring marriage?

Ah, happily ever after! Love triumphs all! Many of you might find these notions as an idea that exists in only movies and fiction. Well, not everyone can become a Marshall Erikson some have to be the Ted Mosby's out there, searching for 'The One'. But, it is about the right person with whom you spend the rest of your life that matters.

Relationships are like flowers in a garden, you have to nurture them with care in order to see their true potential. If scoring a home run is the epitome of baseball than marriage is the home run of relationships.

Yes, some marriages seem to go strong even after 72 years while some last 72 days. Commitments are the bedrock upon which a successful relationship lasts. Achieving this loving and enduring relationship takes time and yes, hard work. Nothing in life comes easy after all.

Now, the question arises what makes a loving and enduring marriage? Is it love? Commitment? Sacrifice? The answer to this question has been troubling many people for decades mow. Conductive researches upon this very subject have been performed by many scientists and psychologists.

You might have seen some successful marriages in your life, be it your parents, grandparents or even friends. You are always in wonder and amazement of their relationship. This might get you thinking what are the secrets of such a happy relationship? Well, readers this is the blog for you. So enjoy!

- **Finding the right person**- most marriages end in a divorce which is a hard fact. But, those are with the wrong person in your life. Until and unless you find the right person, you will feel uneasy with your partner. This does not go to say that love marriages are the only solution. Arrange marriages can turn out to be something you might not expect.

  You will experience a swarm of emotions throughout your life, joy, sorrow, rage, heart break, but with the right person you will have the strength to go through with it no matter what. Getting to know each other's habits, preferences, moods, essentially caring about your significant other goes a long way into a happy and successful marriage.

  The right person is the one with who you are comfortable sharing your experiences, someone you know will be there for you and you know you can blindly trust.

- **Communication**- the most essential tool of sustaining a healthy relationship is communication. Talk out your differences with one another. Instead of sitting in the corner sulking like a child, talk it out like adults.

  Most marriages break down because of a lack of communication skills. Most differences in a marriage can be settled if only you talk to each other openly. Be honest about your feelings and listen to the other person also.

  It is not necessary that you have to talk to settle differences, but talk in general. Tell him/her about your day, ask how their day was. Communication is a basic necessity of every marriage ever.

  Shutting out your emotions will only lead to a big blow up after a point. It's better to converse and be gentle and thoughtful about it.

Shouting is also not a good approach, it is best to keep calm and adapt to the situation.

- **Stop keeping scores**- a vital key to a loving and enduring marriage. Attitude plays a huge part in how you handle a relationship. You might be right about something but going the extra mile just to prove a point is not the way to go.
Do not keep scores of who owes whom. Otherwise, your entire life will blow away while you keep tabs of who said what. Always trying to have the last word in every argument is not essential, sometimes it's best to let go.
It is in your hand how you would handle disagreements. You can be calm and collective for a healthy relationship or be crazy enough to put your ego in between and ruin your marriage. Learn to let of little things which do not really matter. Do not hold something which might have happened years ago and use it in later disputes.

- **Commitment-** committing to each other is the foundation of a marriage. Infidelity is another reason why marriages do not last. Remember why you are marrying the person in the first place. You are committing to each other for life and you have to honor that commitment every day.
Yes this might be harder to do than just write, but that's what it takes to last a marriage. Do not commit only to the initial stages where it is the honeymoon period, but the journey is worth taking till the end of days.

Love is always important but committing to each other is just as important as love. If you have dedication and trust for each other it will lead to a long lasting wedding. This goes for both the genders, committing is the stepping stone to a happy life. Respect your partner and above all trust him/her.

- **Be sure to enjoy couple time**- do not let the passion disappear from your married life. Yes sure, there are jobs, children and families to look out for, but do not forget to spend time with your partner.
  Rekindle the romance even after 50 years of marriage. Who said only young couples can have fun? Surprise your partner with a date night and enjoy your evenings in each other's company.
  For a successful marriage romantic relations with your spouse play an important factor as well.
  Be creative and insert a new dynamic into your marriage to keep things from getting unexciting. Even small gestures can help grow the love you have for each other.
  Do not wait for the other one to take a step; instead you initiate something new and fun.

Being in a marriage is not an easy task and making that a loving and an enduring one is much more difficult. But it is worth it if you find someone to call a friend, a companion and your other half.

How to deal with disappointments in marriage?

Marriage is a journey which sometimes comes with road blocks. This is the way of life. If you are suffering from a bad marriage or some other issues of marriage, you are not alone. There are thousands of others who are suffering from the same issues. While this does not make the pain go away, it can always make the suffering easier.

There are a number of things which you can do to deal with the disappointments. Yes, you don't have to suffer inactively. You need to help yourself to cope with the issues that keep coming back when you are alone. The issues will always creep their way back, until you do something about them.

Don't Fight the Pain

Yes, sometimes fight or flight seems like the only two remaining options. But, sadly, you cannot fight pain. When you fight, the pain will fight back, harder. Remember that in a clash of will and pain, usually pain wins. It will come back when you are not looking, in the most unexpected way.

The other option – flight, well, where do you run from pain and disappointment? You can run only if you are able to make your heart go numb, which is not an option.

So, what do you do? How do you cope?

The best way to deal with pain is by accepting it. The moment, you accept that there are few things in life which you will not be able to change or modify, the ache will lose its intensity. Don't beat yourself for the things you have not done or the things you have done.

Disappointment is an integral part of life. You need to accept this fact. Also, you need to make your heart understand that there will always be another tomorrow. Even if you are disappointed today, does not mean you will remain so forever. Things will start to turn brighter with time.

Time does the healing. So, give yourself time.

Don't Social Media Stalk

To deal with disappointment in marriage, you need to control your urge to visit your spouse's social media profiles. This might not be an easy thing to do. But, this is necessary. The more you look at their lives without you, the more pain you will endure.

This is a poisonous habit. Don't adhere to it. To heal the wounds you need to stay out of touch. This is why – stop visiting their profiles. If possible, deactivate your own profiles for a while. This will stop you from visiting their profiles.

While this might not be the best of the advices, this is an effective way to get away from the issues that keep crowding your heart.

Meditate

Spiritual works have their wonder. People might not have fully embraced it, but, when you follow a spiritual path, you get a lot of insight. The change comes from within. If you are searching for happiness, you need to look within instead of outside. When you sit in silence, you will find yourself capable dealing with all the issues.

The fact is – you are stronger than you think. You have yourself to love and pamper. Frequently people forget this. Meditation is a way to get back to the inner guide. As you meditate, you will find yourself at peace. The most difficult task is to forgive your own self for making the mistakes. Meditation will bring you to the peaceful state where you come to term with the errors of life and come back stronger.

However, meditation is not an easy practice. At times it gets difficult to sit quiet without any movement. Focusing the mind is another difficult issue which you will face in meditation. However, if you keep practicing, if you commit yourself to meditate for a few minutes every day, you will notice the wonder.

Start a Journal

Journal writing is a kind of therapy. Experts claim that journal therapy can change life magically. However, there are people who start writing about the negative things of life in their journal. Sometimes such practice brings adverse effect. When you are suffering this might not be the right thing to do.

So, find a colorful journal. You need to buy one that makes you feel happy. If you are happy with the journal, you will want to get back to it. Now, instead of using the boring blue or black pens for writing, you can get yourself multicolor pens.

Start a positivity journal. Don't dwell on the things that have not worked. Instead, focus on the things that are going well in your life. If there nothing positive going right away, simply write about the future plan. Paint pictures as vivid as you can. This will help your mind to drift away from the present issues. As you keep writing in this manner, you will notice that your mind and your life both are transforming in better way.

Invest on Yourself

The best way to deal with disappointment of any kind is to – create an improvement plan. Yes, you need to remember that – the only person who you can change is yourself. Therefore, instead of trying to change the situation or someone else, invest on changing yourself. There is always place for improvement. There is always place to do better. Join a class if possible. Read self-help books. Start an intense workout routine. There are countless ways to improve yourself. The secret is to feel better, feel happy.

So, create an improvement plan today and act on it. This is one of the best way to steer away your mind from the lingering issues of marriage.

Lastly, remember that no one can help you to overcome disappointment. It is you who can do the wonder. If you are not willing to help yourself, no one will help you. People will eventually get tired of they see you suffer all the time. Instead put a strong front and be your own mentor. People will admire you for your strength and your commitment.

How to re-build trust in your relationship

'Trust' is the base that nourishes all relationships. As a result of TRUST in a relationship, the partners can enrich in kindness, love, honesty, respect, and love. When there is trust, there is no space for major conflicts between a relationship.

What do you think is the biggest problem in a broken relationship?

- Ego
- Trust
- Broken promises
- Cheating partners
- Deep betrayals

These are the most common reasons that would invade marriages and it leads to severe impact.

Undoubtedly, relationships are quite complex, but not every betrayal means the end of the relationship. At times, such betrayals might also strengthen the relationship. Every relationship needs a 'spark' that helps to continue and strengthen the relationship. FORGIVENESS is the key to success!

Do you have problems in your relationship? Are you trying to re-build trust and start a new journey? Here are some tips and tricks that will help you to strengthen your relationship and lead a happy life.

Forgive yourself

The first step toward rebuilding trust is to forgive yourself. Try to understand the situation and know the possible reasons and explanations that lead to such annoying situation, no matter even if they are rational. Broken relationships generally include two ends blaming each other for what has happened. Self-forgiveness would help you learn about the vulnerabilities and the flaws on your end and would also give you every possible way to behave and understand the situation of another one.

Did you forgive him/her?

The second step towards re-building trust is forgiving your partner. Firstly, control all your emotions and make sure you have gained your inner peace to handle the situation. Sometimes, people lack the courage to forgive the partner for their behavior and words. However, in such a situation it is important to concentrate on the relationship you carry and emotional freedom. Learn to forgive and try to focus on the future rather than the past. Try to view the situation from the viewpoint of another person. It would help you understand the situation and the emotion related to it, helping you in forgiving your partner. Take a glance at the good qualities and time spent with your partner if anger comes in between.

Try to trust yourself

If you can trust yourself, you can trust others! If you have gone through betrayal, it is obvious that the fear of emotional devastation, humiliation, and shame could haunt you but overcoming such emotions will help you lead a better life. If a person has betrayed you once, may not necessarily betray you again. Listen to your instinct and believe them. Forget the pain you have gone through and try to refresh your mind with fresh memories. Even if you have gone to physical and mental abuse, it is necessary to forgive the person and forget the experience.

Develop trust in your partner

How could you trust someone who has never supported you? And have betrayed you?

You need to practice the art of forgiveness and ensure you trust your partner no matter whatever the situation may be. Learn to say 'Thanks' and 'Sorry'. Talk, discuss and help your partner understand your expectations. Understand what they are going through and it will help you understand their point of thoughts as well. Trust them, encourage them and believe them. Learn to appreciate their strengths and be supportive and help them whenever they need. Trust is the major factor that will help you strengthen your relationship.

Work on your responsibilities

When you are in a relationship, you need to be more responsible! When your partner is in need, help them, assist them and take care of them. Participate in their good and bad. Try to improve your relationship by satisfying the needs of your partner. Try to adjust according to the needs of your partner. You don't have to change completely buy you can make minor adjustments for your partner. For example, if your partner likes White and you don't, it is perfectly normal to wear white at least one time to satisfy the request of your partner. Small adjustments like these will help you manage your relationship in a better way.

When you are responsible, you need to learn and accept the mistakes, learn to apologize and ensure you can good care of your partner, understand their needs and spend time with them every day trying to understand how they are and what they go through.

Listen and talk carefully and attentively

Being a good listener helps you to have a good relationship. Once you learn to ask forgiveness and is ready to forgive, you need to ensure you listen attentively to your partner. Do not make them repeat the same thing again and again. You need to be smart, use your postures and gestures to greet, say sorry or make any decision. Understanding the posture and gesture of your partner is essential. Learn to have eye-to-eye contact, control your emotions and find out if your partner is comfortable in your presence.

Using good words, apologetic sentences, accepting mistakes, forgiveness is the greatest thing you can do to rebuild your relationship. Maintain an eye contact while speaking, understand their body language, you must be able to say if your partner is happy or unhappy with their simple gestures. Be calm and do not shout in anger. When there's an argument, be silent and listen to what the other person has to say. Make decisions when you are not angry.

Remember, no one is born perfect. Everyone makes mistakes. But re-building trust is a process that includes patience rather than torturing yourself. Just as you took time to forgive your partner and yourself, he/she too would need equal time. it is not necessary to get an instant response every time. Be patience with your process of re-building your relationship with your partner and look for opportunities to grow and make stronger relationships.

10 Things Happy Couples Never Do in Their Marriage

Happiness is something that binds any relationship together. It brings along other elements like trust, love, loyalty and many more which helps in making any relationship strong. And when it comes to marriage, every element is equally important. Marriage is a spicy relationship which includes challenges, arguments, disagreements, happy moments, understanding most importantly love and care. But above all, what matters the most is how the couple avoids all the negative attitudes.

Do you want to be the ideal couple? If you are looking for secret tips, here are something that every happy couple follows. This will help you develop a healthy relationship and a happy family.

1. Stop complaining about your partner to your family and friends

While having misunderstandings, the first thing couples do is talk about the problem with their friends and family. If you want to be happy in a relationship you must avoid talking about your personal things to your friends and family. Remember, not every person would give you a good advice to solve your disputes. There are people who may misuse the situation giving you negative ideas or feedback. It is absolutely fine to fight and have an argument but one must be careful not to bring in a third party into this.

2. Stop comparing your spouse with others

"Hey honey, you know what, the lady next door has bought a new TV. Her husband earns thousand hundred dollars", "Rita's husband takes her for movies every weekend", "John's wife cooks well"

Why should you compare your life with others? Comparing your life and your partner with others would ruin your relationship. No one is born perfect. Every one is unique. You cannot and should not constantly compare your partners with others. Happy couples are those who accept their spouse for who they are and what they do. They do not compare their life with others!

3. Don't snoop on each other

Do you check on your partner's emails, text messages or social accounts? Do you spy on who your partner is talking to? This is something a happy couple would avoid doing. Snooping slowly reduces the trust levels among the partners and at times, misunderstandings may lead to serious issues. Again, this doesn't mean to trust each other blindly, but constant snooping might result in doubting the love your partner has for you.

4. Is there any proper time to express your love?

Why wait for occasions like birthdays, anniversaries, Valentine's Day, Rose Day, etc. to express your love? There is no specific time to express the love you have for each other. Share your feelings, whisper romantic words, whenever it is necessary. Appreciate what your partner cooks for you or buys for you. Thank them and make them feel special all day. Send flower to them on a busy day, send text messages between office meetings, take them on a date, give surprise gifts. and make the bond much stronger than before. So, stop checking out the calendar to search the right date.

5. Say NO to social media

Happy couples are those who are not in social media! Undoubtedly, today every piece of happiness is shared on the social media sites by people. Whether you buy a pizza or go for a movie, or fight with your partner, you post it online. But if you want to be happy, limit your posts on social media. Sharing everything on the social media might craft you like the best couple or perfect couple, but investing that time with each other would help in improving the relationship in real. So, limit your access to social media for sharing your emotions and best moments.

6. Don't Avoid dates after marriage

Marriage brings a number of responsibilities like work, commuting, kids, and other responsibilities and the couples lack required time for each other. This slowly reduces the spark of romance and intimacy among the couples. Don't let this happen. Spare some time for each other and look for dates, movie plans, day out, long drives, etc. All these would help in strengthening the bond you share.

7. Give space to each other

There are many couples who stick to each other thinking this would help in enhancing their relationship. But the fact is that providing each other with some space would work better rather than staying with each other 24/7. Let him enjoy some time with his friends, as you share some time in kitty parties or shopping with friends. This would refresh both and increase the urge of wanting each other as they stay apart for some hours or days. Allow each other to enjoy their individual life too independently.

8. Stand beside and not opposite to each other

Do you compete with each other in various aspects? If the answer is yes, you are surely on the wrong track of being a happy couple. Rather than competing with each other, stand beside and work as a team to defeat even the worst situation in life. Instead of getting jealous, help each other to get success. This would help in getting the quickest way out of any difficulty with ease.

9. Practice to forgive

No relationship is perfect. Every couple suffers from fights and misunderstandings where they might lose their temper. During such a situation, instead of hurting each other or oneself, look for ways to deal with the issues and forgive each other. Of course, at times, the situation can be too harsh. During such problems, hold patience and give some time to understand the moment by getting into each other's shoes. This would prepare you to forgive your partner and begin a new journey of togetherness.

10. Make sure you don't ignore finances

Financial problem is something every couple would have to face in their marriage life. And most of the husbands are found hiding the financial situations from their family and wives to avoid extra pressure. However, the correct part is to discuss the financial needs and goals which is carried out by happy couples. Communicate and distribute financial responsibilities to protect financial matters from getting worse. No matter whether both are earning or either one of them, discussing money matters to get the right solution on time.

No couple is happy and perfect from the beginning. Constant efforts, mutual understanding, and trust on each other are some of the pillars walking on which the couples gain the title of the happy couple in their marriage life. What do you think? Will you stand by your partner or walk against to find solutions?

Best ways to build mutual trust in your marriage

Love is not the only thing that will help your relationship. Any relationship grows strong with wonderful blessings like love, respect, friendship, understanding, mutual trust and much more. TRUST is, however, the vital thing in any relationship. A friendship grows when you trust your friend, a business grows when you trust your customers similarly, trust between two individuals results in marriage and relationship.

Try replacing TRUST with fear and suspicion and you will ruin your life completely. When there is no trust, there's fear and a feel of insecurity.

When it comes to conveying mutual trust, communication is the best way to exchange feelings and emotions. But building mutual trust is not an overnight task. It takes time, and once it is obtained, it is equally important to maintain the levels through honesty and interaction.

Are you also looking for the best ways to build mutual trust in your marriage? Try some of these couple exercises that might help you in strengthening your bond with your partner.

Discuss your negative experiences

Couples always share their happy moments spent with friends and families. But have you ever dared to share a scary or negative moment or experience? If your answer to this question is 'No', you need to open up! Try sharing your negative, sad or scary moments or experiences one day. This would increase the honesty levels in the bond you share. The couples should not only discuss the cherishing experiences but should also share the scary secrets which would also increase the trust among them. Stay honest with each other and let your partner know what you have gone through.

Can't you spend 20 minutes of your time with your partner?

Go for a walk with your partner, join the same gym, help them with groceries or pick them from their office. Hold hands together while walking, hug each other whenever you get a chance, start the day with a kiss and a warm hug. Be kinds, soft and romantic. Look into the eyes of your partner while talking, hold their hands while talking about anything serious. Try to spend time together and gain each other's trust.

Work on decision making

Most of the relationships struggle due to improper decision-making situations. While taking any kind of important decision, make sure both of you are having equal roles in the decision. Discuss the matter before coming to any solution. Many times, the husbands carry out the decisions and the wives are not also involved in it or vice-versa. Avoid this process and carry out mutual communication with a peaceful mind to come to the right solution. This would improve mutual trust on each other in your marriage as you talk on any matter and make decisions.

Admit if mistakes occur

No one is perfect. Mistakes can be committed by anyone anytime. And admitting the mistakes would be the best thing to build mutual trust stronger. It is next to impossible to meet the expectations of everyone and hence, forgiving partners would surely help in avoiding blunders. Confess your mistakes and try to avoid them for developing mutual trust. Once any mistake is committed, it might lead to small problems in the initial stage, but would surely help you build a strong relationship in the future.

Confess your love

It is often observed that as time passes after marriage, the couples miss the spark of love due to responsibilities, children, and much more. They take their relationship for granted and lack the love and intimacy they should have. Take an initiative and start confessing the love you have for each other. Tell why you love each other, take time from your busy schedules and spend time with each other. Express your love in different ways that are comfortable for both of you. Get more feel of togetherness rather than loneliness for increasing the trust you carry.

Accept the importance of your partner in your life

The relationship works when both the partners perform as a team. But if there is competition among the partners, this is surely not going to help in increasing trust in each other. There are people who self-promote themselves for their efforts in the relationship. They simply look for areas of their interest and think themselves to be supreme in the relationship. Instead, know the importance of your partner and respect him/her. Be grateful for their efforts and their presence in your life that has helped in keeping the relationship working and also enhanced the level of mutual trust. Look after their needs and interest.

Power of unity

When there is mutual trust among the couples, emotional attachment develops on its own. Be emotionally available for your partner when they need you emotionally. When the couples are heartily connected with each other, they understand each other's requirements and needs too. The power of unity would develop in a situation when the couples emotionally stand by each other in good and bad situations and work as a team in getting out of it. The power of unity would aid in growing mutual trust among the couples building a strong relationship.

3-minute eye contact

This may sound silly, but making an eye contact for around 3 minutes is one of the best trust building exercises. Practicing this exercise would connect the couples emotionally and also would be helpful in developing the activity of mind reading. For this, a seat on your couch, bed or any place you are comfortable in and set a timer while you gaze into each other's eyes for 3 minutes. The activity might seem to be funny, as in the initial sessions you might laugh too at each other, but it would slowly help in building trust on each other for sure.

Trust is an essential ingredient for any relationship. Hence, continue nourishing your relationship by actively participating in the exercises to build mutual trust while kindness and love would in return follow its way into your relationship.

What makes life partners the best partners?

"While you are busy looking for the perfect person, you will probably miss the imperfect person who could make you perfectly happy"

What according to you defines a 'best partner'?

What qualities do you look for in your partner?

Do you have an idea of how your better half should be?

Everyone has different dream. Some wants their partner to be beautiful and smart while the other one wants to be lively and bold. Some wants their partner to have a lot of humor sense while others want a serious person to be their better half.

You take a lot of decision in your life and among the most important decision, choosing your LIFE PARTNER is one of the most important decision that you will ever take. And everyone has a huge list of qualities that you look for in your partner. But the true fact is that, however small or big your list is, it is difficult to find the perfect girl or boy who suits your qualities. True relationship is all about expecting less, respecting each other and accepting the partners as they are.

Can we define a "Best Partner"? If you'd ask me, I would say 'NO' because what is best to me might not be best to you!

However, here are few things I have discussed in this blog that talks about a perfect relationship and life partner.

Do you connect with your partner easily?

Connection or bond is much essential in a relationship. If you find connecting or communicating with your partner difficult, or if silence is the only thing that surrounds you both when together, you are sure with an incorrect partner. Look for a person you can easily get into a conversation with. This would make you free from inside to talk on any kind of issue, topic, interests, etc. together without getting irritated. So, find someone easy to connect with.

Should best partners have same interests?

You may like adventurous but your partner might like spiritual travel. This doesn't mean you have a bad partner with Not-so-matching ideas! If your partner is ready to travel with you on an adventure travel and if you can travel with them for a spiritual holiday, there's a perfect balance in the relationship and you can equally enjoy. Having common hobbies will me more interesting but if you can adjust with each other's interest it's much appreciated.

Share a strong friendship bond

The base of a healthy relationship is friendship. There are many couples who were best friends before they tied a knot. So, while going for initial dates or meetings, check whether you are able to build a strong friendship bond with him/her or not. A solid friendship would surely lead to a strong relationship as both would be easier knowing each other well.

Reliability

Life is too tough and when it comes to a relationship, reliability is an essential element that is required among the partners. What is the reliability level with the person you want as your life partner? Do you trust in sharing every piece of your life with him? Can you rely on him for every small and big decision of your life or work? If yes, this is surely the best partner you can spend your life with. Remember, the best partner would never leave you no matter wherever you stand.

Is he/she a good listener

Being a good listener is not only limited to listening to the words. It includes the unspoken words and the silence too. Are you able to understand what the individual wants to convey without too many words? If yes, you can head towards best partners. Again, this also includes sharing how you took their message and the clarification regarding any point in communication. Having a good listener reduces the chances of miscommunication and misunderstandings in a relationship.

Focus on the communication skills

Along with being a good listener, the individual also needs to be a good communicator. Communication here means paying attention to every word uttered along with the tone used which doesn't change the meaning. This also includes avoiding aggressive or irritating words that can lead to disputes. The role of a good communicator should involve words, comments, or talks that makes the listener feel comfortable, understood, respected and cared. So, choose one who is good with clear and effective communication.

Is he/she looking for quick marriage?

Engagement is a phase when two unknown people are given a chance to observe and know each other deeply. The time span of an engagement was priory a year which provided both the parties with required space and time to know every detail about each other. No doubt, things today are moving quickly, but six months to is a fair time to answer yourself whether he/she is the best partner you can have for a lifetime. So, if you are insisted on a quick marriage, take a u-turn as this might be a sign of something unwanted.

It is good to look for standards

Considering the standards of each other's family is surely not a bad idea before finalizing everything. As today, people are insisting to have marriages in similar families with similar standards, the problem is solved to a great extent. However, looking for your partner in some other strata but not completely out of the mark is also advisable and adaptable. So, give slight importance to that standards too while selecting your best partner.

Loving oneself

Do you think the individual would love himself as he would love you? If the answer to this is no, the person is not made for you. Look for someone who would stand for himself at times if you are not there. He/she should not be dependent on you or your company for going against unfavorable and unknown situations. They should be comfortable and totally secure with themselves without you around. They should be confident and have similar trust levels as they have on you on themselves.

Again, along with all these, sexual attraction, romance, sense of fun, values, and much more which would get you the best partner. No doubt, human beings can never be best partners totally every time, but if your partner is having many of the qualities as discussed above, you are sure to lead a happy life ahead.

Why do people say "Honesty is the best policy" especially, in building a successful marriage?

There have been never-ending debates on whether honesty is the best policy for having a successful marriage. Just as there are people who think honesty and transparency are essential for a successful marriage, similarly, there are some who think slight dishonesty is also required to build a successful marriage. According to a survey conducted with married people, around 30% of the couples have admitted hiding big to small secrets from their partners, while around 8% also have a secret account in the bank.

Undoubtedly, every partner or individual comes with some loop falls and some stronger sides, but when it comes to a successful marriage, being transparent with each other is much affordable as dishonesty would not only lead to reduced trust and love but would also lead to serious issues like divorce. Be it a small matter or a big secret, dishonesty would surely harm the bond you share with your partner.

Here are some reasons why dishonesty would not be tolerated for a successful marriage.

It creates a never-ending chain

Yes, dishonesty is something that would take you deep down in your relationship leaving no hope or way to get back your position in your partner's eyes. The first time you carry out any such task you might feel harmless, the second time it would be little easy for you, and slowly, you would get habitat to do it with ease and comfort. This chain would begin with small issues and would end up with dangerous consequences that can lead to horror situations. So, understand the situation well and help you partner grasp it too without any kind of dishonesty in words.

Remember, the children are watching you

When you are dishonest, you might think that no one is watching you. But wait, check if your children are observing you or not. And if you carry out any such task in front of them, you are setting a horrible example for them. They would hear you or watch you doing so and would perform the same mistake in the future. Even though they wouldn't expose you or talk about it to others, it would surely damage your credibility in their minds with a severe negative impact on them. So, next time you feel to carry out any kind of dishonest task, remember you are watched.

It reduces the trust levels too

Trust and honesty go hand in hand. Once your partner would come to know about your dishonesty, the levels of trust would automatically get down along. No matter whether the matter was small or big, once dishonesty enters the action, your partner would lose trust in you and it would definitely be difficult to gain the trust again. This would make things uneasy and full of tension until trust is rebuilt in the relationship. Once the trust is lost, the relationship would also lose the love slowly. Hence, if you are thinking of building mutual trust, make sure you are working with honesty and avoiding dishonesty.

Disturbs the goals of the family

If you have taken part in setting specific goals with your family, dishonesty is surely going to damage them. When goals are planned, the family works hard for achieving it, but due to dishonesty, you move on your way which can lead to a stressful situation for the family. Such plans basically include monetary goals, breaking rules, and much more. Dishonesty separates you from other members of the family as you walk on your own path and this can also lead to the division of the house. Dishonesty henceforth also damages the unity of the family dividing the house, emotions, and love they have.

It would shatter confidence into pieces

Most of the time, the couples hide good things from each other. They avoid sharing their feelings and in return gift their partners with anxiety and hurt. Talk to your partner if you find someone more attractive or are willing to see any kind of change in them for a good reason. Revealing your feelings would increase the confidence levels in the relationship and would also be helpful in building intimacy in the relationship where your partner would want to win you back. Dishonesty or hiding your feelings can lead to serious issues in the future which can be destructive too.

Lacks emotional needs

For many couples, honesty is the base for their emotional needs. It develops a feeling of security in the relationship which makes the bond stronger. Come forth and discuss your thoughts, feelings, dislikes, likes, habits, personal secrets or history, future plans, daily routine, etc. which helps in the development of mutual understanding too. Again, while discussing all these, make sure both of you are calm and respectful to each other. Honesty provides required emotional needs the couple would require and dishonesty is surely going to damage it or reduce it.

Makes you lonely

Of course, no one would like to spend the entire life alone. The idea itself is a big flop. But for this, it is important to have high honesty levels among the couple. There are times when you shall shatter down, get emotionally weak and insecure too. In such a situation, you are sure to need someone to hold on, someone you would trust blindly, someone who is honest to you. If you are honest to your partner, you are surely never going to be alone to face the difficult situations of life. So, don't feel shy, speak it off instead of blaming as dishonesty would leave you alone to face every bad moment.

In the end, working out life together can at times be little difficult, but honesty in your behavior, words, and actions is surely going to gift you with a successful marriage. Counting on each other would help you work on every good and bad moment together when honesty and transparency are along with you and your soul mate.

How to build emotional intimacy even after years of being married?

Emotional intimacy is an association that goes past the physical, holding two people— mentally, emotionally, and spiritually. An emotionally connected couple can share their emotions and feelings openly with another—she looks for your certainty, and you her. There's a realizing the other individual has a sufficiently deep understanding of you to have the ability to see your perspective. If you and your life partner are progressing towards the emotional connectivity or hoping to make your relationship stronger, you may find the following blog helpful.

What is emotional intimacy

Emotional intimacy is commonly characterized as a closeness in which the two partners feel secure and adored and in which trust and communication flourish. When you are candidly close with your life partner, you feel as though you can see into the other's spirit, knowing their expectations, dreams, and fears and understanding them at a deep level. Relationships minus emotional closeness is regularly portrayed by an absence of trust, poor communication, secrets, and hidden feelings.

Recognizing a lack of emotional intimacy

Now and again, couples don't create emotional intimacy in the first place or lose it sooner or later. The two partners need to take a shot at keeping up and building closeness. If you are a depressed spouse, you may have a portion of the attributes of an emotionally unavailable man.

Frequently, couples don't perceive the signs when emotional intimacy is inadequate. For instance, a lady might be in shock when her better half announces that he needs to leave the marriage. Thinking back more firmly throughout the long periods of their marriage, she may review times when there was an emotional distance between them.

How to increase intimacy in your marriage

If your marriage is by all accounts lacking in emotional intimacy, there are various things that you and your partner can do to strengthen and develop emotional intimacy.

Figure out to be vulnerable

Vulnerability not just forms trust, it is likewise fundamental to forging an emotional connection. However, getting to be open to one another may not come effectively for a few couples. Vulnerability— the capacity to express one's needs and wants sincerely and openly— carries a specific risk. Justifiably, past rejections may make one hesitant to take a risk.

If you and your companion consent to begin opening up to one another, credit to you both! Take it slow and share a tiny bit at a time. Continue encouraging and supporting one another, and in the long run, sharing your thoughts and emotions straightforwardly with your mate will turn out to be second nature.

Build Trust

Realize that it requires time for a man to put his/her trust in someone else, and be totally vulnerable. The process of building trust is a vital one—not only in the big things but also in the little ones as well. Making and fulfilling a promise to complete a task, for example, is a little thing that says a lot about your dependability and reliable quality.

Spend some quality time together

Try to give each other more quality time and keep spending more time together. When you begin doing things together, you get the opportunity to appreciate the opportunities for holding and increased communication. To zest up your discussions with your life partner, listen mindfully and keep up eye to eye connection. It makes your life partner feel important and adored.

Get physical

Touch can expand the feeling of closeness. Set aside a few minutes for sexual intimacy. Take time to appreciate one another. Being intimate, frequently encourages a feeling of closeness to a person, bringing to you a positive development as you move in the direction of creating emotional intimacy.

Express appreciation and gratitude

Make your life partner feel that he/she has had bought a difference in your life. Sometimes, a couple can become distant when there is no criticism, response or appreciation for the work of love. Try to express your gratitude and appreciation to your partner frequently.

Keep the gadgets away

Think about turning off the PC, TV, video game, phone, and tablet when you are together and invest some energy, talking, sharing, and looking at each other directly into the eyes. One device that numerous effective couples use is keeping their mobile phones silent and dropping them in a little basket or box once they are home and consenting to abandon them off for no less than an hour or two when they are together.

Be safe for your spouse

After years together, couples unavoidably realize what may hurt their partner. Kind and cherishing partners who avoid hurting each other, help each other feel adored, respected, and safe. When we make the earth ok for our life partners, emotional intimacy discovers its place.

Spend maximum time together

It very well may be hard to find time together as a couple. Having youngsters in the home can regularly amplify that trouble. Try to spend 30 minutes each evening regularly with your life partner after the children are sleeping. Deal with assignments together, similar to dishes and shopping for food, so the things can complete quicker and you can get to know one another as partners.

Read a good book together

Reading a book together and talking about what you are reading can be a decent vehicle for expanding emotional intimacy. There are some extraordinary books about strengthening marriage that you can read together, however you can likewise pick a novel, life story, or a book about a common interest. The way that you are reading together and discussing what you read can strengthen the trust and communication part of emotional intimacy, allowing you to share your emotions and experiences without passing judgment on one another.

Look for a balance between yourself and the couple

The most strongest marriage connections have two reliant partners. Everyone has rich leisure activities, a professional life, or a social life, and they meet up to put resources into the marriage relationship. An excessive amount of harmony can be an awful thing if it deprives the relationship of the energy and experiences that interdependency brings. So, try to take part in some great self-care, and enable your partner to do likewise. And, after that meet up as a protected and trusting couple.

Setting up passionate closeness with your partner may require some serious energy, yet take heart, the time and effort you both put into one another will definitely pay off!

How to spice up your sex life after long years of marriage?

Sometimes the most loved-up and head over heels in love couple can go through periods when the intimacy happens rarely. There are obvious reasons behind this period- the birth of a child, financial setback, office work related stress, and much more. But a lack of emotional intimacy for a longer period of time can wreak havoc on any deeply committed couple's love life. Therefore, it is imperative to prevent your relationship reaching a drought level and start making plans to bring the spice back to your love life. Start by making sure that both of you are completely healthy, and there are no physical issues, and if that seems to be the case, the affected partner can see a doctor for a better insight into the sexual problem.

Moreover, it is equally important for both the partners to be on the same page about going gets out of the intimacy drought and if there are any relationship issues that needs to be resolved, you can always see a couple counselor or a sex therapist to figure out the problem. This can be done using medication to treat problems like anxiety and depression, and through stress reduction techniques and sex therapy sessions. Following are few ideas to help you spice up your sex life:

Attempt new things

Be curious to attempt new things. Try something you and your partner have not tried for a long time or have imagined doing it. Be experimental. You can try new sex positions or have sex other than the bedroom. It could be your shower, kitchen, back seat of the car, backyard, or in the hotel.

Utilize your words

Obviously, this can mean speaking dirty if both of you are so engaged and realize that you'll see it exciting to hear your cherished one express certain words or expressions amid sex. Be that as it may, it additionally implies talking up about what feels better and what doesn't. Ladies, specifically, can be shy about offering direction to a lover amid sex.

In the meantime, however, by not communicating how or where you need to be touched, for instance, you don't just cheat yourself of pleasure you likewise deny your partner of the excitements of realizing that the person has made you feel great. If expressing words are really excessively troublesome, attempt physically directing your partner together with your hands.

Put some sex on the calendar

Spontaneity can be misrepresented. If you and your partner are continually keeping an eye out for the ideal minute or for the state of mind to strike, you might stick around a ton, so take a seat together and make sense of when you both possess energy for sex and write it into your timetable.

Also, don't simply pick a date and time—make progressively specific arrangements: Choose a place, a room, even a fantasy you might want to carry on. By setting the stage, however much as could reasonably be expected, you can seed expectation that can bloom into all out excitement when you come together.

Use smartphones

Your telephone can possibly be used a thousand times for arousing than the techiest vibrator if you use it right. For whatever length of time that you realize your partner will be able to get messages in private, send sexts and erotic photographs of you or what you'd like to do with him or her when you two would be alone. Furthermore, when that occurs, switch off your gadgets with the goal that you focus around turning each other on.

Send a spontaneous sext

Rather than 'what's for supper?', take a stab at adding some sex to your writings by communicating something specific about you need to do when they return home. Try not to be hesitant to get specific. Review details concerning one of your most smoking encounters, portray an outfit you'll be wearing — or perhaps send a pic of yourself in it. An unforeseen hot message to your partner is an extraordinary method to assemble that pressure for the duration of the day, so when they return home, you both realize it's go time.

Role-play outside the room

Role play doesn't simply need to be constrained within the bedroom. Both of two can dress up, go out, and arrange a "one-night stand. During the one-night stand, act like outsiders the entire night: different names and backstories, and flirt as though you just met. Towards the night's end go home together.

Make your own erotica

Get a diary to pass between both of you. One individual begins the erotic story and other partner picks up from where they had left out. If you need to make it extremely explosive, consent to no sex for a few days while you're composing your steamy story. Before the week's over, you will be eager to get your hands on each other.

<u>**Best ways to improve your communication with your partner**</u>

"Marriages are made in heaven", they say! Well, it may be or maybe not. Ultimately, marriage is nothing but a relationship that brings two people and their families together. Good marriage depends on a lot of factors like emotions, trust, communication, and more. It's common for married couple to go through different phases of emotions – good times, bad times and sometimes even worst times. The common factor that plays vital importance during each phase is communication. Communication can be a blessing in disguise or the worst curse. During rough times, the communication style will be completely different when compared to the communication style during happy times (such as a vacation or a normal weekend).

It's essential for married couples to maintain a healthy and honest communication. Troubled communication is never good for a healthy living. Ever felt the difficulty to open up and speak with your partner? Or a situation when you were really for it and your partner did not respond back? Also, don't forget – over communication is also not a healthy way of communication as it could lead you into trouble. This article will list out the best ways in which you can have improve and maintain a healthy communication with your partner.

1. Maintain a face to face communication

Make sure you actively listen to your partner during a conversation. Even if there is a disagreement of opinion, make sure you hear out your partner fully. Acknowledge the discussion and then try to give your answers for the disagreement or if there was a question posed at you. While responding, make sure you put out facts in a subtle way. Never interrupt when your partner is speaking. Maintaining this culture will cool out most of the burning fire. It's more important that you maintain a face to face communication when you want to convey something important.

2. Make the right time

You may have lot of things in mind that you want to communicate to your partner. It's crucial when and how you put them through. Find a time that is best suited for you and your partner. Make sure there is no distraction during the talk. Try to assess the situation before opening up the conversation. Home is your best place to have the perfect conversation. But if you've had the worst of experiences at your home, choose a neutral place such as the park or a drive that will ease the temper for both of you.

3.   Never put the other person into a defensive state
Don't be harsh and accuse your partner. This gets them into a defensive state. Ask the right questions in the right way to generate the perfect answer. Don't use judgmental words! This can result in increased temper and unwanted course of actions in case of heated arguments. Also keep your interactions simple. For instance, if you want to tell about your day in the office with the client, don't use the technological syllables that you use back in office. Tell it in a nice way so that your partner can easily understand your point of view and move on from the issue in hand.

4.   Don't dig the past history
Always ensure your communication stays in the present. Don't make general statements like "you're *always* like this! how many times have I told you in the past?". Forget the past and make it history. Connecting the past with present is equivalent to digging your own grave! In case of an argument or a discussion, don't quote instances from the past as it the chances are more for it to backfire and increase the intensity of the discussion into a heated argument. This could also make your partner feel guilty for something that happened previously and that you've overcome over time.

Complement each other

When there is a chance, try to complement your partner. "You look great in this dress today!", "You look gorgeous in this makeover"- such words can mean a lot and make the day a lot better. As you get busy in your daily life, don't let complacency take over. Never hesitate to show back love! Compliments need not be verbal. Even the faintest of touches with pure love could mean a lot. This can be so much reassuring of how much you mean to your partner.

5. Have an open and honest communication

Being honest and open in a relationship makes life more easy. Even a single lie can ignite a whole world of problems. If you feel the slightest of disturbances within you, make sure your communicate it to your partner. Keeping your emotions within yourself is fine, but for how long is the question. Unless you communicate, there are all possibilities for the emotion to burst out in all forms (anger, hatred, and more). Let off the little penny issues, but if something keeps you bothered always, speak it out! Don't feel accused when your partner throws his/her emotions on you. If the mistake is on your part, apologize to him/her rather than finding excuses, or trying to provoke your partner. After all, no one is perfect!

6. Maintain a positive body language and a neutral tone

During a conversation, make him/her get the real feeling that you are fully attentive to their claims. Maintain eye contact and respond back. Lack of eye contact means you are not interested to hear your partner out. Maintain a low and natural voice tone. Raising your voice can lead to an emotional disturbance in your partner and result in a heated up argument.

Communication is not something new. It's the same what we do in our daily life. When it comes to family life, there are times when situations take control and it's important you don't get over the situation. Don't let emotions and expectations overrule you. It's crucial to remain calm and communicate in the right way to build and maintain a healthy relationship. These communication tips will help you communicate effectively with your partner and lead a happy family life.

How to deal with an angry spouse?

Every married couple go through ups and downs in their life including different emotions like love, happiness, frustration, disappointment, anger and lots more. Out of these, anger is the most contagious and powerful emotion. If not controlled, anger can cause a real turbulence in your family life. Especially in a married couple's life, excessive anger can lead to a traumatic life style and depression. A 2009 study reveals that anger contributes to deep depression in your partner, and doubled the rate of having symptoms of a heart attack.

It's crucial for either of them to strike a balance and understand the cause of the anger. That's not easy as said! Anger has the tendency to bring out your emotional self. The biggest challenge when trying to control the situation and calm down your spouse is actually not getting angry and control your emotions. The moment you let it go, things tend to get out of control. It's hard to balance this situation but if dealt in the right way, you can have a better relationship with your spouse. Here are some strategies on how best you can deal with an angry spouse.

1. Effective Communication

Communication plays a major role in a family relationship. When your spouse is angry, it's important to know the best way to communicate. Use words that will make them feel comfortable. Do not use provoking words or try to emotionally threaten them. This will make them feel more insecure. Use a soft language and try to understand the cause of their anger. Engage in a healthy discussion as this will calm down things and give you the space to think and find a solution for the problem.

2. Keep your calm during the conversation

When your spouse is angry, try to be calm and assess the situation. Don't let the situation take control. Staying calm potentially reduces the heat of the discussion. Never return back anger when your spouse throws anger on you. This adds fuel to the fire. The consequences will be worse with unexpected twists. The calmer you remain during the argument, faster the time for your angry spouse to calm down. Once there is silence after the thunderstorm, sit down with your spouse and try to address the issue in hand.

3. Be patient and compassionate

When your spouse is angry and accuses you of something, remember it's lot more than what's on the face of it. Hidden within is their feelings and emotions that get pumped out in the form of anger. It's nothing but a sudden state of their mind when they feel things aren't going their way. Anger is a transitional state of emotional weakness. Don't lose your cool when your spouse gets angry on you. Be patient and compassionate; and share lots of positivity to them. Keep in mind, never be sarcastic or critical. This could heat up more anger in your spouse. Saying a simple sorry or giving them an assurance will keep things under control and heal the situation smoothly.

4. Acknowledge and listen; do not provoke

Make your spouse feel that you are actively listening. Also if you sense that your partner is angry on something, go ahead and try to understand the problem. Do not provoke him/her. Chances of a heated discussion is very high and can put things out of place. Try to keep the issue within the context of the situation.

5. Don't take angry discussions personally; but there's a limit

If your spouse shows their anger on you, not always it means that you are the reason for it. Anger could be due to lot of mental stress and disturbances. Remember that during an argument, not always you must accept the blame or tolerate any abuse from your partner. When things get out of control or go beyond your boundary, make it clear to your spouse to stop it right there.

6. Hold a personal discussion

Finding it difficult to live with an angry spouse? Set aside time and have an open discussion. Try to have the discussion at the earliest after the first instance of a fight or a misunderstanding. Leaving it unnoticed will give your spouse another chance to repeat the instance. During the discussion, let your partner know that anger will ruin your marital relationship. Open up and try to understand what problem your spouse is going through. You might not be able to find a solution immediately, but this discussion will give you an idea of what's in your spouse's mind.

7. Influence your spouse

Create a positive influence on your spouse; let him/her know your feelings when they show their anger on you. Shower love on your partner and tell them know how much they mean to you. Make them understand your feelings and at the same time try to understand the cause of their anger.

8. Get a counselling

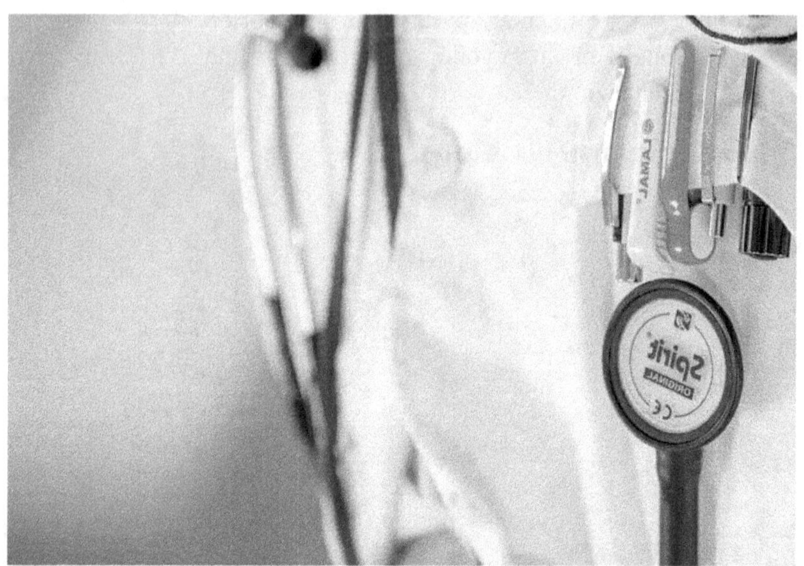

If you feel things are out of control and problems continue to persist in your marital life, make sure you visit a doctor or a counsellor as a couple. Otherwise let someone whom your trust the most know about your problem. Tell them and get a reasoning for the cause of the problem. Appear for multiple sittings with the doctor to help them understand your spouse's situation and suggest precautionary techniques. If your spouse doesn't agree to meet the counsellor, you go ahead and still make an appointment. Tell them how much you get affected by your spouse's anger.

These strategies can help you deal better with your angry spouse and also stand a chance to make them realize their problems. Never return back anger for anger. The best way to overcome your spouse's anger is to stay calm and let the situation subside, then try to understand the cause of the anger and find a solution for it. By doing this, you are bound to maintain a healthy and happy life.

Here's how you can make your marriage an enduring marriage?

After the honeymoon period is over, the reality usually strikes in. Marriage is the kind of journey which begins with a lot of expectation, but, usually ends with utter disappointment. While that is a reality in the modern era, there are a lot of things which can be done to alter the situation.

If you want to cling to the butterfly that flutters inside your stomach each time you look at your spouse in the wedding night, you need to work a little on your marriage. The best thing about the marriage is – the relationship can be improved. All you need to do is – be willing to fix the rough spots that frequently arise in the lives of the married couples.

Appreciate Your Partner

When you are married to someone for a long time, you usually start taking the parson for granted. Nothing about the spouse you have adored so much in the past seems great anymore. This is the first problem the married couples make.

So, rather than getting settled into a routine so comfortable that you forget to acknowledge each other's presence, make sure to remind yourself the sweet moments you have spent together in the past.

Appreciate the love you have once felt for each other. If possible maintain a marriage journal for yourself. Write down the loving memories and read this to your spouse when you two have got nothing important to do, or, when you two are on vacation.

Written words sometimes work its wonder. Remember that everyone likes to be appreciated no matter how old the relationship is.

Focus on the Little Things

Life is a collage of moments. This is why – you need to focus on doing little things for each other. Even little gestures of love can make miracle happen. So, try to make a cup of coffee for your spouse when they are working without having to ask for it. Even a little shoulder massage can be a great gesture which will help you get closer to your spouse.

The idea is to make them feel loved. If you are doing big things like bringing home expensive gifts or taking them out to lavish dinner, you are doing great. But, there is nothing more romantic than bringing home a red rose, maybe cooking meals for them. It will touch their hearts if you make little efforts to shower your affection on them.

Encourage them

Well, does your spouse have a hobby or a passion? Make sure to stand by them in the time of need. To pursue passion, one needs to go through a lot of trial and errors. There will be moments of doubts. There will be times when they will question their ability. However, if you stand strong in the moments of doubt or struggle, you will not only be appreciated, you will be rewarded with a strong and loving marriage. This is why – always try to be the cheer leader for your spouse. However, yes, there is a however, here. You should try to judge their work with honest opinion. If you think there is place for improvement, you must say so. It will make your spouse produce better work.

Have a Positive Attitude

Positivity can win anything. Yes, it can win your spouse as well. If you are going through a rough time in your marriage, you need to cling to the positive mindset. The secret is to look at the bright side of the marriage. Even if you two are fighting a lot lately, you are still together. This matters a lot. Yet, the experts say that just because you are being positive, does not mean you will totally ignore the problems. This will never make the problems disappear. Rather, the problems will come out in the open later on with all its animosity.

Therefore, don't ignore that you two are fighting. Try to work on the issues that are creating the differences between you two. A little compromise might help you overcome all the problems. A little discussion might get you to the solid ground. You never know what might work out. So, keep an open mind when it comes to making a lasting marriage.

Don't be Shy to Talk

More than often married couples fall into the state of silence. This can be engulfing and can ruin a relationship. Most of the relationships fail because people don't want to talk about it. If you are going through some kind of doubt, you must talk to your spouse about it.

There are times when talking spouse becomes difficult. If you want to have a lasting marriage, you need to be open to discussions. Together you two can solve the problem which you are facing. There is nothing like a team work. You need to remind yourself that you and your spouse are on the same team.

It is not about Winning

People measure life in the terms of winning or losing. But, marriage is the kind of journey where winning or losing does not matter. Here the relationship matters. If you want the love to last forever, you need to give up your desire to win all the time. In fact, winning an argument does not have to be a priority, like making the first move to end a fight should not be a reluctant approach. Be the first one to break the silence and the fight. Be the first one to say sorry. You would not lose anything if you make this a habit. You would not be inferior if you bend a little to support your marriage. Think about it.

Seek Professional Help

If you think that the marriage is slipping out of your hand, if you think you are unable to deal with it anymore, you should not be shy to seek professional help. It does not matter whether the problem arises on the 2nd of your marriage or 20th year. Sometimes talking to a professional counselor works better than seeking advice from friends who are going through the same problems.

How to make time for each other amidst your busy life?

A relationship is based on making time for each other. It is an important part of a successful marriage. Yet, often due to the haste of life and lack of free time, people end up ignoring the most important aspect of marriage – they don't give each other time.

While it is understandable that modern life demands hefty amount of time, you cannot deny that marriage is an essential journey. To make it successful you need to work on it as well. Making time for each other is one of the essential tasks and you need to be creative to squeeze out time for your spouse.

Create a Calendar

Like everything else, you need to give it importance. To make time for your spouse you need to freeze dates. A calendar will help in this task. Make sure to get yourself a planner where you create your schedule days ahead.

Here you need to block days for your spouse. Once you have blocked the days, you need to chalk out plans to spend time with your spouse every day. Even if it is for half an hour, you need to do it.

After you have filled the calendar, you will attach essentiality to it. Even if you don't follow the calendar totally, you will at least make time for your spouse every day. The idea is to make yourself understand that marriage is an important part of life. While you are chasing success in your professional life, you need to chase success in your marriage as well. Also, make sure to keep the calendar within reach. This way, you will be assaulted by guilt if you fail to stick to your plan.

Motivate Yourself

Sometimes professional gatherings seem more inviting than spending time with your spouse. This is one of the problems which all the married couple faces. However, if you succeed in motivating yourself to spend time with your spouse, you are sure to succeed in making time.

Think of all the glorious things you are going to do with each other. Also, plan surprises for your spouse. Think of the ways you will make your spouse smile. This is a great way to motivate yourself to work hard and make time for your spouse.

If the trick fails, think of the loving times you two have spent together. This will help you make time for your spouse.

Discuss with Your Spouse

Yes, this is another great way to create time for each other. Sometimes people make plans without consulting the other. Often this leads to disappointment. Rather than opening yourself to this situation, make sure to talk to your spouse about the dates you are blocking for family time.

Once both of you agree to spend time with each other, you can go ahead with planning the dates. Also, discuss about the daily family time together as well. The idea here is to make the family time special. Once you value the family time, you will want to keep the dates no matter what.

Work Out Together

So, both of you are too busy to even spare a day for family time? No problem. There are ways to spend time with each other even if you have the whole day blocked.

Create a morning exercise plan together. Even if you two go for a run every morning, make sure to do it. You two can join a gym together as well. This will help you spend a lot of time with your spouse. You two can create fitness goals together as well.

Join a Class Together

There are countless classes which you can join. If you think making time for your spouse is getting difficult, make sure to join a class with your spouse. This can be anything – from yoga class to creative writing class, anything will do the work, if you are willing to commit to making time for each other.

Plan a Date

This is a romantic way of spending time with your spouse. Make sure to take turn and plan a date for your spouse every month. This should be a mystery date which you plan solely without telling your spouse. If both of you take turn to plan dates for each other, it will be two long and romantic days with each other. Make sure to enjoy the time together.

Journey to the Past

Once a month, make sure to talk about the past. Discuss about the time when you two were young and foolish. If possible take down the scrapbooks where you have collected the photographs. A tour to the past will be better with mementoes. Or, you can create a memory journal as well. Here you can write down about the time spent together. Try to collect all the good memories in the pages. Then later one read this to your spouse.

You will treasure the time reading the journal to your spouse.

Cut Down Television Time

Well, this might be required if you really want to spend healthy time with your spouse. The amount of time you spend before the television, can be spent with your spouse. So, try to cut off some time that you spend watching the daily soaps. If you watch four shows, cut it down to two. The rest of the time you can spend with your spouse.

Or, you can watch the television together. Find shows that interests both of you. Watch these shows together rather than fighting for remote.

Night Time Date

Because both of you are busy in your life, make sure to utilize the time after dinner. Surprise each other night time treats. Make sure to have a chat with a cup of coffee every day. This is should a daily habit.

Lastly, try to make time during the day for a couple of video calls. Technology is there to help you erase the voids. So, try to make use of the technology and make video calls when you cannot be physically present with your spouse.

Proven ways to avoid miscommunication in your marriage

Communication is one of the most vital pieces of a relationship. What and how things are said, assumes a huge role in the constitution of the relationship. Indeed, even in the most advantageous of connections, there are contradictions. Two individuals have diverse encounters and points of view on things and keeping in mind that they might impart and discussing it, what is being said can lose all sense of direction in interpretation.

Remarks are made now and forth, one individual gets observably furious and their partner says, "Quiet down." Two little words that when said amidst a warmed exchange resemble lighting a match and dropping it in a puddle of fuel. For the most part, things heighten before long and it's troublesome for individual A to understand why individual B is disturbed and individual B can't completely verbalize why it is irritating.

In this way, stop and think for a minute. While those words alone are not proposed to be negative or hurtful, in this setting they have a not really constructive outcome. Saying this amidst an argument can regularly feel contemptuous and request driven, like stating "quiet down" which most can concur isn't at all helpful in this situation. So, what do you do about it?

Communication is the by-product of connection but not vice-versa

Obviously, issues in love connections don't happen on the grounds that individuals are excessively inept to make sense of sound judgment strategies for communication or too brained damaged by the experience of marriage to recall how they used to communicate. But, it's deceptive to state that individuals in intimate connections have communication issues by any means, however, it can feel that way to them in their dissatisfaction and misery. It is progressively exact to state that couples in upset and troubled relationships have connection issues.

Communication in love connections is an element of a passionate relationship. At the point when individuals feel associated, they communicate fine, and when they feel detached they convey poorly, paying little mind to their selection of words and communication strategies.

Before you communicate

Try not to consider how to motivate your partner to do what you need or, if you favor the code word, how to "convey" with him/her. Or maybe, ask yourself few questions first, such as:

- Would you like to feel emotionally connected with your partner?
- How curious, you are to learn about your partner's point of view?

- Do you care how they feel at this moment?
- What do you cherish and respect about your partner?

Having addressed those inquiries, choose whether your connection could easily compare to the subject of your communication. You should convey that you will love and respect your partner whether she/he agrees with you or not. Anything shy of these downgrades the association - it's not as essential as what you need to discuss, in this way ensuring negative reactivity.

4 Ways to prevent miscommunication in the marriage

Listen eagerly: Be totally mindful. Most false impressions happen in because we don't listen completely to what is being said. For text contents like messages, read carefully each word. The reason being, if you have different contemplations in your brain, they can irritate and cripple you to totally or effectively understand what the other individual truly needs to pass on. Also, in some cases, there's a whole other world to what is being said. You have to understand the hidden real importance behind the words.

Observe carefully: Guarantee you don't miss any visual cue that can add to the data conveyed and make it complete. Watch how you convey your words. At times, things sound awful, however they look fine, and the other way around. Attempt to know the expectation of the individual through these cues. The goal is commonly more essential than the content. You might frequently get annoyed with the tone utilized, and assume it is being utilized deliberately. Keep your mind open and clear, and don't make assumptions.

Have clear thoughts: Verify your thoughts properly before you give them the privilege to impact you. You ought to clear up your questions, assuming any, there and after that. Do this before the worm of misconception finds the opportunity to sneak in and breed in your psyche.

Check if the non-verbal communication of the individual, outward appearances, and different elements run with what is being passed on, and the manner in which you see it. Attempt to affirm if the perception framed in your brain effectively identifies with the cues displayed. Resist the compulsion to respond immediately.

Assess your observations and confirm: See whether what the other individual is conveying is the equivalent or different from what you have understood. If you see, it isn't in concurrence with what the other individual is stating, at that point you have to realize this could lead to misconceptions.

It is then better to honestly talk you mind, and request a clarification. Have persistence. Give time and chance to the individual to clarify. Have discussions if conceivable, before making a hasty judgment, responding, and making a hue and cry! Regardless of whether you do as such, let the other individual know the exact purpose behind your responses.

Tips to Avoid Being Misunderstood

- Think before you talk
- Go for face-to-face conversations
- Pick your words wisely and avoid using any ambiguous ones

- Properly use emojis like smileys, exclamatory signs, or expressive shortened forms like LOL.- while messaging or SMS, and in your talks
- Frame your sentences well, and check the tone
- Consider cultural differences since same words may be utilized in various contexts
- Try to reply earlier, because staying quiet for long time breeds misunderstanding
- Clearly express your intentions and convey the right meaning
- Communicate effectively

Keep in mind, life is short. No one can really tell what's in store tomorrow. In this manner, clear up issues now, and don't keep such imperative issues pending. Try not to keep any misconception in your head. Continuously try to abstain from misconception, wherever possible. Communication is a vital factor to avoid misconception. Thus, make a point to talk frequently and consistently with the individuals who matter to you. At the point when two individuals — with various identities from various families and foundations — get together, clash is inescapable. However, good couples can walk through the clash constructively. Keep in mind that you're in a similar group. Make sense of your sentiments, express them tranquilly and listen eagerly to your partner.

How to beat stress and anxiety in marriage

Stress and anxiety can be damaging to a marital relationship. Yet, marriage in itself a stress provoking journey where problems come and go. If you are not sure how anxiety and stress can cause damage, this article will give you a clear idea.

Anxiety Ends Trust

When anxiety and stress occurs, trust usually is the first thing which gets affected. At the time of anxiety, people usually forget the need to give space to a relationship. This creates suffocation and strain marriage. Remember that when you are anxious, your partner too is anxious. One of you need to control the problem to save the marriage.

Anxiety Creates Panic

At the time of anxiety people usually get panicky. They start behaving differently. You will not even know when your behavior changes and how many hurtful words you are using.

Anxiety Reduces Acceptance

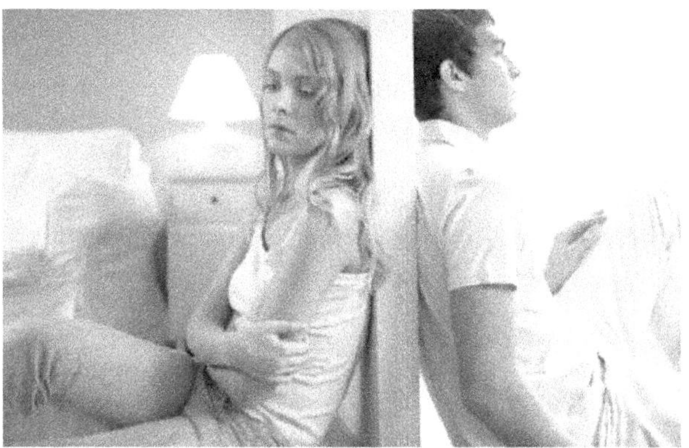

People usually start acting selfishly, when they are under stress or anxious. This usually create problem in acceptance.

So, now, you know why you should try to combat anxiety and stress. However, there is a question – how do you combat these two poisonous elements. What do you do to keep them at bay so that these don't affect your marriage?

Experts claim that there are ways to fight anxiety and stress. You can do it if you are willing to save your marriage.

Listen

Well, this is the best quality of a human being. People usually hear words, they don't listen to the inner meaning of the words are carrying. If you want a successful stress and anxiety free marriage, you need to practice listening. This does not mean you will have to do everything your spouse says. This means you just lend your ears to what you spouse is trying to convey to you.

Listening is the best gift you can give to your spouse. Lack of communication can kill a close relationship. When communication gap occurs, people usually start to drift apart. This also creates trust issues. This is also the first step towards a broken marriage.

However, only listening will not diminish the stress. You will have to acknowledge that you have heard what your spouse has said. Also, you will have to send signal that you are willing to take action accordingly. Even if you are not willing to take action, you at least need to explain why it is not possible for you to act accordingly.

Listening is a simple act. It does not cost you anything. However, the result of patient listening is great. Once you start this practice, you will see the transformation in your marriage.

Don't Judge

Judging someone is a damaging thing to do. This is one of the problems which damage marriage. This is why – you need to control your urge to over judge your partner. If they are trying to do something good for you, it is essential that you accept the gesture. You need to make your spouse understand that you appreciate what they are doing for you.

In case, your partner is trying to make your day wonderful, try to participate in the event rather than being cold and distance.

Don't Bring the Past

People usually damage their marriage by bringing the past. This is a bad habit. You need to forget the past and move forward. It does not matter how much your spouse's action has hurt you, if they are making an effort to salvage the mistakes, you need to accept the good gesture.

Practice Meditation

Meditation is a useful practice which comes with immense benefits. If you want to get the stress level down, you need to practice meditation. This is a proven way to combat stress and anxiety. If you are going through stress and anxiety, you need to calm your inner voice so that you can give your hundred percent to your marriage.

This is why – therapists suggest that people should practice meditation daily to keep their stress level down. You can practice this with your spouse so that both of you can spend some quality time together while working on the difficult issues of marriage. Make friendship with silence if you really want to lead a healthy marriage life.

Improve Yourself

To lead a healthy married life, you need to work hard. It is true that you should pay attention to your spouse. But, you should pay attention to yourself as well. It is important that you stick to an improvement routine. Pay attention to your fitness and healthcare. This will help keep the stress level down. You will find yourself bubbling with positive energy. Also, you will be able to make your spouse happier when you feel happy from within.

Daily running or walking has great effect on body and mind. This is why – have strict routine for yourself.

Have a Hobby

It is important that you have a life of your own. You need to have things to share with your spouse. Hobby plays a great role in keeping a marriage happy and pleasant. Also, when you are involved in your hobby, you done usually dwell on the unpleasant aspects of marriage. Therefore, find something you love to do. It can be reading, writing or singing. Anything that keeps you in a positive can be taken up as your hobby. This will improve your thought and keep the stress away from your life. Therefore, find something to do in your spare time today. Cut off some of the television time.

Pause and Ponder

When something is not going right, you need to ponder why it is not going right. For this, you need to be alone time to time. It is essential that you keep a diary. It will help you record the events of your life and later reflect upon them. Diary writing is the kind of therapy which the therapists prescribe. It will help you fight stress and anxiety. You will feel light and positive this way.

Lastly, don't be ashamed of seeking professional help when you cannot take care of the stress and anxiety yourself.

10 Things to do to make your spouse feel special

More often than not, we tend to take our partners for granted. Especially after marriage, the little things we used to do for each other starts waning down. Doesn't it feel bad and sad at the same time that the romantic relationship you used to have is now going down the hill. Well, nobody is to be blamed. But yes, you sure can take up the responsibility of making your partner special. It doesn't have to be Valentine's Day for you to tell how much your partner means to you. Waiting for occasions to express love is just like waiting for the rain to dance. If you're unsure about how to make your spouse feel special, here are 10 things you can adopt today! You'll be happy to have done this to your partner and we're sure your partner will be too. Read on!

10 things you can do today to make your spouse feel special

1) Plan on a surprise romantic date

Many a time, people tend to lose interest in asking their spouses out on a date after marriage. Think about it. Why does this change happen? What has marriage got to do with going out on a date or not. It's nothing but the shift in your mindset. The shift in mindset from 'How do I make him/her feel special?' to 'We're together now. There's no need to make my spouse feel special.' Seeing the lack of purpose is often the major reason behind why some partners stop asking their partners out. The little butterflies your partner will have when you ask them on a dinner date isn't something that must only be reserved for the special dates. Make an attempt now and ask your partner for a romantic dinner date.

2) The little things you do still matters, even after marriage

Little gestures of love and care like helping your partner with their work, the household chores, paying up of the bills, asking them if they'd like an ice-cream outing etc matter, even after marriage. Nothing has practically changed after marriage except for the fact that two people have tied knots. Nothing else, really. So, don't stop yourself from doing the little things you used to do. Your spouse will appreciate your efforts.

3) Make them feel appreciated

It goes unsaid that every person has a need to be appreciated. Everyone deserves an appreciation for the great world they build or being in. When's the last time you told your spouse she looked beautiful? Or when was the last time you told your husband he looked great? Assuming that your spouse already knows you appreciate him or her is no escape to not telling them how you feel. If you like something about your spouse, let them know! Make them feel appreciated and celebrated.

4) Show gratitude for the efforts your spouse is putting in

One major mistake many people make in their relationships is to take their partners for granted. Sure, your partner loves you. That does not mean that it's an obligation for them to do things for you. You ought to be thankful and grateful for the little and big things they're doing for you. Things as simple as washing your clothes or cleaning the bathroom you use together should not be taken for granted. They're doing it out of love for you and they deserve all the respect and appreciation for doing so.

5) Touch them more

Touching your partners bonds your relationship in ways you cannot think. Touch needn't always mean sexual touch. A touch of care and affection too can bring so much warmth in the relationship. Caressing your partner, cuddling them when you're roaming about and other small physical gestures of care will surely make your partner feel special.

6) Sending them gifts is still a great thing!

Many couples tend to stop sending gifts to each other once they get married. This is a huge mistake. It lessens the intimacy in the relationship. If your spouse loves flowers, or chocolates, or some delicacy, or a silent walk by the park, do it for them. Your marriage shouldn't put an end to these things you do for your spouse. Try to recall when's the last time you gifted something to your spouse? Go to a gift shop and pack something special for your spouse and send it to his or her way with a special personal note.

7) Do things you love together

Your spouse may love to listen to his or her favorite music album back to back, or a watch a thriller movie, or a romantic number, or may be watch a cricket match, or just take a long drive. Whatever it is, I'm sure you know what your spouse loves doing. Take time to do it and ensure you do it together. When partners start doing things they love together, it builds a great ever lasting bond between them.

8) Ask them how they feel

Asking your spouse how the day went or how are things at work or how is their family doing is a great gesture of showing how much you care for them. Assuming that everyone is fine is not cool at all. To make them feel special, you need to show them that you care about what's happening in their lives and that all these details count!

9) Make your partner feel heard

Making your partner feeling heard goes a long way in making them feel loved and secure in the relationship. You don't have to be a Messiah trying to provide solutions to everything they're talking about. You just have to lend your listening ears to them and that's enough to cheer them up. Especially with woman, all they want from their spouses is a good attention span when they're speaking of their problems. And some empathy, of course. So, really listen to them and make them feel heard.

10) Be authentic and kind

Being kind isn't an idealistic gesture but a necessary one. Little acts of kindness like doing the dishes or washing clothes or making that pitch in the peak hour for your spouse will make your partner feel that you've always got their backs. It is very important to establish this factor in every relationship. Be authentic in what you do and show kindness towards your partner. It's not only the world that deserves your kindness, but people around you too!

5 ways to lead a happy, contended and fulfilled marriage.

The honeymoon period of every marriage comes with a shelf life and more often than not, it soon starts deteriorating day by day and by the end of one year of marriage, most couples lose the fluttery butterflies of anticipation and excitement. But does that have to be so? Certainly not. There have been many couples who've endured long lasting years of happy, contended and fulfilled marriage. What are their secrets? If you'll know them, you'll realize that they're so simple to do. But that's the thing! Most simple things are so simple to do that people forget why they must be doing it. Just being conscious of doing these simple things is the trick. Here are 5 things you can do to lead a happy, contended and fulfilled marriage. Read on.

5 simple things to do to lead a happy, contended and fulfilled marriage

1) Appreciate each other for all the little and big things you do for each other

Most couples tend to take their spouses for granted after marriage. There is a person who's always there to take care of me and there's no big deal in that - This is the line of thought many people truly believe in. How healthy is it for the relationship? Very unhealthy. Taking your spouse for granted is equal to taking the whole relationship for granted. It's a slow poison that'll eat up your relationship slowly until a point you no longer feel loved or appreciated, and that flags for the end of your relationship. To avoid such mishappennings and to match towards a long lasting loving and enduring relationship, do not take your partner for granted and appreciate the little and big things your partner does for you. This keeps them going and helps them in letting know that you respect and value their actions of kindness towards you.

2) Deal with your arguments constructively

Arguments and misunderstandings are part and parcel of every relationship. That should not mean that you give up on your relationship, throw your hands in despair and do nothing about it. Figure out ways in which you can deal with your arguments in a more adultly fashion and a more mature way. Do not throw tantrums at each other during arguments or fights. Remember that people may forget what led to a fight but will never forget how it made them feel. Talk to your partner openly about the arguments and have a more positive outlook. Listen to what your partner has got to tell and never use destructive statements while fighting. Getting back at each other will not help too. Understand that there's a misunderstanding and try to break the misunderstanding, not the relationship or your partner.

3) Don't just be there for each other, take care of each other

Being there for each other to run errands at home and to help each other with basic things is something almost all partners do. Long lasting and loving relationships do not end at that point. Taking care of each other is extremely important too. Smallest of the gestures like asking your spouse about how his or her day went can bring the warmth in your relationship. Care and truly care for your partner, from remembering the special dates to taking care of your spouse in sickness.

4) Work on increasing both emotional and sexual intimacy from time to time

Emotional and physical intimacy, both are quintessential for maintaining a good relationship. Ignoring either of them can take your relationship downhill. There is no wrong in putting in conscious efforts to increase the emotional and sexual intimacy. It's a myth to believe things will always be great magically! Minds work in mysterious ways and there's a reason things used to happen 'magically' and why they stop happening later. Simply put, it is because in the initial stages of relationships, people tend to put in more conscious efforts to make the relationship work and somewhere down the line, it gets distorted. When is the last time you put in 'effort' or did something special to increase sexual or emotional intimacy? Take steps today to increase intimacy.

5) Put in conscious efforts to make your spouse feel special and loved

Taking your spouse for granted is the worst thing you can do in your relationship and it comes with guaranteed failure. Appreciating the efforts of your spouse for every little and great things they do for you lets them know that you're not blind to their actions and thus helps build a great bond between the partners in the relationship.

Best ways to apologize to your partner

If you've been hitched or in a serious relationship for any time period, you definitely realize that there is no such thing as the perfect relationship. Everybody falters. Everybody makes mistakes. In any case, committing mistakes is a piece of what makes us human. All things considered, there comes a period in each relationship when you realize saying sorry can have a significant effect on your relationship.

Regardless of our best intentions, there are times in relationships in which one or the two partner is thoughtless with words, where sentiments get injured, when outrage is unreasonably uprooted, where there is cold-heartedness to other partner's emotions, where we do or say things that we regret or that causes damage, and much more.

In some cases that implies making genuine, enduring change, and to be very frank, that is a troublesome activity. Particularly in case you're set in your ways, or in case you're not used to trading off. It's an expertise that takes practice, however, you'll get it down. Here are some fundamental steps to manage you through the ideal expression of apology to your partner:

Check your tone: An exaggerated statement of apology might work as another shovelful of soil on your relationship's grave. It's as offending as it is chafing, and it doesn't resolve anything. In case you're not prepared to apologize, or you don't mean it, don't exacerbate the situation with a conciliatory sentiment brimming with attitude. At the end of the day, take a look at yourself before you bring more damage to yourself. It's totally OK to take some time to think or chill after a difference. Giving a vacant conciliatory sentiment to your partner will hurt your relationship.

Recognize your partner feeling: Most of the time, when we feel hurt, we likewise truly need to feel understood. Regardless of whether you don't figure you did anything wrong, it can just make your relationship more grounded if you set aside the opportunity to understand why your partner is angry or harmed rather than simply giving a sweeping statement of apology. Attempt to see things from their viewpoint, and consider that they might likely have distinctive emotions and points of view on things than you do. Truly try to identify with your partner, in as caring and find a way out from the gross situation.

Get to the root of the situation: Hurt emotions are typically more profound than only a response to indiscreet words or a neglectful error. Perhaps your partner is angry at you since you were late for a night out on the town again. In any case, that is only the basic issue. It's most likely that your partner is truly feeling like they are not a priority, or that you're not putting as much effort into the relationship. Don't simply concentrate your statement of regret on the mix-up (the delay). Dive into the more profound issue (your needs). This is the genuine contrast between a negligible statement of apology to conceal any hint of failure confront and a mindful apology to resolve an issue.

Demonstrate your partner you are sad: Use "I" explanations to apologize to your companion. Show that you've disguised your misstep and gained from it, and saying things like, "Well, in some cases you do the same thing," simply wouldn't help or sound genuine.

Request your partner's forgiveness: As hard as it sounds, when you request for forgiveness, you should be prepared to hear "no." Your life partner may not be prepared to excuse you yet, and that is alright. You can't request quick forgiveness, so if your partner says they aren't prepared to excuse you yet, you should have the capacity to take it in a walk. Despite the fact that it tends to be agonizing, disclose to them that it's alright and that you get it.

Give your partner some time to think: Depending upon the level of your slip-in, it might take your partner some time to forgive you. This is alright, and it's essential for you not to surge them through this procedure. Clarify that you're sad, and after that wait for them.

Focus on not committing that error once more: The best expression of apology on the planet won't have a touch of effect if you continue committing similar errors. So, make a plan to keep that from occurring. For instance, if you neglected to take care of an essential task (i.e. paying the telephone bills), set reminders with the goal that it won't occur again. This will demonstrate your partner that you consider their feelings important and that you're focused on making your relationship work.

Be prepared to apologize on different occasions: Sometimes one sorry isn't sufficient. To demonstrate real penitence, you can ask for forgiveness more than once and offer consolation to friends and family, particularly for genuine mistakes.

Prepare a plan for change: Once you've apologized, and gotten to the core of what's extremely wrong, you have to determine things by making an important plan for change. This could be something as straightforward as saying "I will counsel you before I make extensive buys" or as intricate as saying "I will do all that I can to modify my calendar and ensure our relationship is the best need in my life." And despite the fact that you're the one doing the saying 'sorry' there's a lot of space for bargain here, and changes from your partner too. Making an activity arrangement indicates you're both dedicated to one another's satisfaction and the accomplishment of your relationship. It makes an expression of apology considerably more significant on the grounds that it's supported by activity.

Show you mean what you say: There's no reason for making a plan to change your wrongful conduct in case you're not going to finish. Try to back up your words with meaningful actions that will make your partner believe in you.

One of these languages of expression of apology will echo the strongest emotions from you. Furthermore, likely, a slightly different one will resonate a strong vibe with your life partner.

How to strike a balance when you and your spouse have varied interests?

You've heard the well known proverb: Couples who play together, remain together. Like different pearls of ancient wisdoms, it's true till this day! Partners who routinely participate in commonly enjoyable exercises are bound to have solid, loving relationships and are less likely to sign divorce documents. Actually, common interests functions as a sort of barometer for a relationship's state of wellbeing The more common exercises partner can have, the stronger the bond is between them.

It's anything but difficult to perceive any reason why this is so. Life partners with common interests put in hours together. They feel upbeat in one another's quality. They have bounty to talk about during supper. They build up an interpersonal network of like-minded people. They have a great time arranging, doing and repeating occasions they've shared. They fill a mystic memory box with common recollections.

Common interests are as fluctuated as the people who appreciate them. A few couples look for experience. Others like painting or watching movies. Still others adore doing humanitarian effort or going to spiritual retreats. There's no correct method to play together. The key is that the two individuals must keep themselves engaged.

Basic interests additionally change through the span of a relationship. Exercises that might be ideal for twenty-year-olds may not be ideal for individuals who have had hip replacements. Individual interests falter, too. A couple may appreciate breeding cocker spaniels for various years at that point proceed onward to something unique they haven't attempted.

It's additionally suitable to approach one basic enthusiasm from contrasting perspectives. A spouse may like skiing in the Rockies, while his less athletic wife appreciates spa treatments and shopping at the resort.

If you are feeling like you and your significant other share nothing in common, here are some promising thoughts to encourage your marriage.

It's alright: You don't need to have similar interests to have a decent and flourishing marriage. Marriage is about selflessly cherishing, supporting, and thinking about each other, putting the other individual's interests previously your own. At the point when each partner does that well, the wellbeing of the marriage follows. You don't have to adore the things they cherish, yet you do need to cherish them.

Value your differences: Try not to cherish them, notwithstanding your differences. Cherish them as a result of them. There are incredible preferences and qualities that accompany being extraordinary. You are with somebody who takes a look at the world from an alternate edge. Take a look at the distinctions as resources because it will help both of you have a 360-degree viewpoint.

Do soul searching: Ask yourselves, "What unites us delight?" Sometimes the appropriate response is quite obvious. On other occasions you'll have to dig more.

Respect each other's interests: You don't really need to do similar things, however, respect what they like and urge them to do it. When they are accomplishing something they like, it gives them a chance to relieve pressure and bring delight. Talk about it. If you get some information about it, that is always better. Concentrate on what it does to them and the delight it brings.

Explore new things: There are a million new outcomes. Attempt new experiences and interests together. Ensure it is something that neither of you has done previously. There will be plenty to discuss and you may very well discover something that both of you appreciate doing together. Hold onto it as an experience or giggle together about it being a test.

Make a new list: On different sheets of paper, record what every one of you may jump at the chance to do. At that point look at your thoughts. You might be agreeably amazed at how comparative your dreams are.

Look back to your dating years: Review what you did when you were first together. Those exercises clearly spoke to you once previously. Maybe those early interests can be tidied off and shared once more.

Do something new: Search out exercises that excite your interests that you've never attempted. Take bridge lessons at the grown-up school. Join a choir. You may find another passion. In any event you'll have to attempt it.

Schedule a time to play together: Try not to let unending overscheduling interfere with your relationship. Block out a piece of time on your shared schedules. Even better, make a common date with the goal that you generally spare time for one another.

Be inventive: Sometimes, having no answer sounds interesting. You have to think outside the social box. Maybe you volunteer to create a new landscape while your better half performs in a community play. Or on the other hand, you can also offer to bring pasta to your better half's softball outing. You'll be engaged with the activity. You'll be cooperating as a group.

Have a decent frame of mind: Whatever you do together, do it with an adoring heart and an agreeable attitude. In case you're sullen and angry, you've nullified the whole point. Conclude that you'll have fun around with your partner, and at that point, put on your best smiling face forward. There's such a great amount of laying on your common participation. After all, your marriage is in question, you need to find the best way out!

Taking a break is imperative for a marriage: For spouses who continually sublimate their very own necessities to those of her family, husbands should need to urge them to take a small scale get-away from their activity. In any case, with the goal for her to do as such, he should guarantee her that her home and family will be fine, and a major piece of that confirmation incorporates going up against the duties she's attempting to let go off. Spouses should need to remember this is very their best advantages. A split far from obligations will make spouses more joyful, and when wives are upbeat, husbands by and large feel a similar way.

Thinking about Divorce? Here's what you need to know!

A standout amongst the most hopeless occasions throughout your life is the point at which you don't know whether you should remain married, or get separated. In case you're considering divorce, odds are, you know the great desolation of not having any desire to remain hitched, but rather being reluctant to get separated. However, being stranded somewhere close to being joyfully married and getting separated can take numerous structures.

You can be stuck in a troubled marriage, yet at the same time perplexed that getting a separation will just exacerbate your life. Or, on the other hand, you can be confronting the appalling reality that your companion took part in an extramarital entanglement. If that is the situation, you might think whether separate is your just, or best, alternative. You may likewise be in an alternate position through and through. Your life partner might be the person who broke the news that she needs a divorce. Presently, you're contemplating divorce, but, not because you need to stop it!

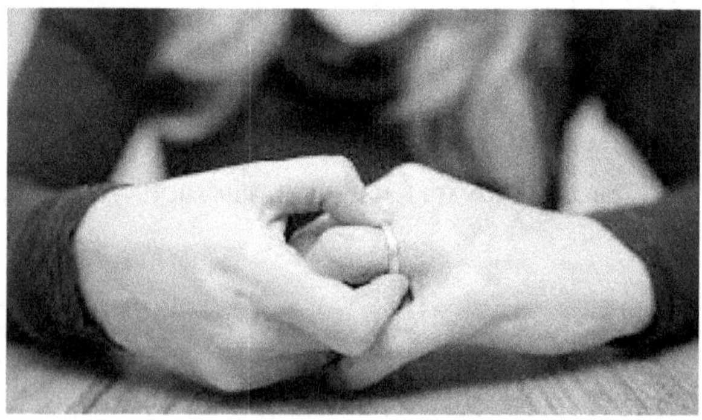

If any of this sounds like where you're at, read through the following things that can help. Simply pick the ones that are appropriate for you.

Line up your encouraging group of people: We see you saying, why it is important? Indeed, even people who get along extremely well, once the papers are recorded with the court can end up feeling alone in light of the fact that loved ones might be hesitant to favor one side. It occurs, and that is the reason conversing with a couple of close partners (companions or family) and requesting their help can give you more certainty if you choose to continue.

Get counselling: If you've effectively taken a stab at advising couples or individuals, and came up void when searching for motivations to remain married, you can skirt this tip. Guidance, if you've not attempted it, is to support you, regardless of whether you choose to part up or not. Being certain this is what you can require digging and who preferable to enable you to dig other than a trained professional? A lot of undecided individuals start counselling as a preliminary measure, and you're being wise to think about it.

Gather and protect financial reports: This might sound funny, but it is an important thing to hold on to. Make copies in the event that you stress they could bafflingly vanish. Try not to be ridiculous in your approach. Keep it very simple. Numerous couples begin focusing on smoothing the route for a final separation say, "We're focused on parting things fairly." Sometimes, that is valid. In any case, if not, you'll secure yourself by squirreling away copies of of bank and retirement accounts, debts, assets, credits and other financial. Reserve them with a relative for protection.

Need a new car? Get it now: Numerous individuals discover this tip somewhat odd, yet it bodes well: amid what could be a long and strenuous road to separate, the court may not permit both of you to make a critical buy or sell significant resources since they're viewed as marital property. Further, you wouldn't be the principal individual to be forced to bear a once-agreeable, prospective ex who chooses that exact retribution is something to be thankful for and profiting an issue is the most ideal approach to get it.

Disclose to your partner: When you've chosen it's a great opportunity to isolate, you have to tell your partner. Have a transparent discussion regarding, why you need to get a separation and to settle on a joint choice about brief living plans and care for your kids. Do your best to respect your life partner – it will help you both keep away from an extensive and drawn-out separation process. In case you're stressed over making a scene, think about holding this discussion in an open space. In case you're a lady and worried for your well being or your kids' security, and don't think a respectful discussion is a choice, your initial step ought to be to visit a nearby women's shelter.

Tell the kids: Educating your children regarding the separation is typically the hardest part. Caring guardians will talk about this among themselves first, and will attempt to concur on the best way to tell the youngsters what's going on and accentuate that each parent will proceed to love and care for them. Keep in mind that the most ideal approach to have a full and solid association with your youngsters, and their kids, in the years ahead, is to demonstrate to them that while you and your ex still have respect for one another. Youngsters pick up the way you treat the other parent and it's vital to set a genuine example.

Set out your terms of separation: Any couple can separate, but you need to have a mutually agreed separation terms set out in a paper before proceeding on signing the legal papers. A divorce is the lawful advance to dissolving a marriage. So if the parties are in a custom-based law relationship, and were never legitimately married, they won't require a separation. Just married individuals require a divorce.

Regardless of whether you're married or not, except if there is nothing to manage, it's most shrewd to set out the terms of your separation in a separation agreement. Once in a while the understanding is clear and should be possible without struggle. Different occasions an agreement can be challenged and require significant negotiation. In any case, it's better for parties to work out their own understanding than to have a preliminary and pay legal advisors to battle it out for a judge to settle on an ultimate conclusion.

Pick up the best lawyer for your situation: Every couple is unique. Every divorce is, too. Choosing a highly-qualified divorce lawyer will make it easier to deal with the grave situation and will also help you to be comfortable and feel confident, knowing that the relationship between client and lawyer is very much legal, individual and private from the very first moment.

Try not to keep privileged insights from your lawyer: When somebody strolls into a confession booth or looks for spiritual direction from an imam, what great would it do to unburden oneself if the inquisitor avoids truth? You should conclude that you'll completely uncover everything to your lawyer, regardless of whether you feel disgrace or blame. It will make your situation light and will enable your lawyer to get more insights into the matter.

How to forgive your partner without jeopardizing your opinions?

In each relationship there are probably going to be times when your partner will get things done to you that you might view as hostile, insensitive to your sentiments, or just imbecilic. At the point when that occurs, your reaction is, somehow, unsurprising. It's normal to end up offended, hurt, irate, or have other comparative responses to this apparent damage.

Not every person will translate indistinguishable words or deeds from destructive or disquieting; some are thicker cleaned or won't think about a few offenses literally or genuinely. It can rely upon the specific circumstance. For instance, an impromptu remark from your partner, for example, a joke to the family's monthly expenses may be overlooked or even taken as amusing in a few circumstances, however viewed as a noteworthy insult in other times.

Having the capacity to excuse and to relinquish past damages is a basic instrument for a marriage relationship. Moreover, having the capacity to pardon is an approach to keep yourself sound both emotionally and physically. In fact, excusing and giving up might be a standout amongst the most essential approaches to keep your marriage up securely.

1. Rethink the reasons you're together

Return to the start. Ask yourself: What attracted me to this individual in the first place? What characteristics did they have that I discovered important? What made them so astounding? What's more, would they say they are still? Reconsidering the reasons you met up helps you to remember the motivations to remain together, and this reinforces your officially existing establishment. Ask your partner what they adore and don't adore about you; be available for productive analysis and personal development.

2. Convey

There is a correct way and an incorrect method to convey. The correct way is asking your partner an applicable inquiry, tuning in to their reaction, at that point offering your conclusion. The incorrect way is overpowering your partner with your worries and stresses when they stroll in from an especially long workday. Practice viable discourse by connecting with your loved one in an advantage discussion. Make inquiries that issue to them; individuals open up when you ask about their day, an imperative task, their emotions, and so forth. When you've tuned in to what they need to state, offer your side of the story. Avoid overwhelming discussions in upsetting occasions, and particularly in the warmth of feeling. Quiet down, at that point, approach the subject once more.

3. Do something different together

Maybe both of you have a most favorite restaurant you haven't visited in a long time, or you can come back to where you initially experienced passionate feelings for? Being in a physical space where you have powerful memories of solid connection can reignite energy. Or on the other hand, you can have a go at something you've never attempted. The energy of something new creates serotonin and dopamine in the mind. It doesn't need to be something phenomenal; notwithstanding sitting on a recreation center seat viewing the kids play as you clasp hands can be supernatural if love exists. Interestingly, you stop looking at taking that vacation, or attempting that new spot, and finish on your goal to reconnect together.

4. Cut out external impacts

Frequently it is the outside voices that saturate our private connections and mix danger. Try to understand who's playing a negative role in your relationship and focus on keeping that individual's energy out! Keep your relationship as private as could be expected under the circumstances and disclose as meager subtleties as you can. Don't consequently concede your adoration hardships to other people. Odds are they don't hold the solutions to your issues. Open up the portals of communication rather and confess your worries to your partner.

5. Pardon one another

To pardon is to segregate - from the sharpness, outrage, and enmity keeping you away from the advancement with your partner. Let go of the negative feelings that is keeping you from genuine forgiveness. Advise yourself that whatever occurred, occurred, and that there is no motivation to drag the past into your future. Waiting on harmful recollections just propagates them. Be careful that forgiveness is a procedure, not an outcome, so perform little, day by day acts that are intelligent of your expectation to pardon.

6. Tell the truth around a certain something

We, as a whole, hold a couple of mysteries that would profoundly hurt others if they discovered. This is typical. Certain things ought to just be kept within ourselves. In any case, genuineness can trigger thoughts in your partner's mind as they would think of you. Conceding one secret or error to your partner may make them need to open up, as well.

7. Set limits with one another

Furthermore, keep your word! If you set a standard for your partner, set a comparable one for yourself too. This implies, if your partner guarantees not to remain out late on a Saturday, you ought to comply with a similar standard. A relationship is a two-way road. Tell your partner sincerely what you might want them to do (or not do), at that point be set up to acknowledge the limits they set for you, as well. Keeping up a relationship inside agreeable limits maintains a strategic distance from contentions, blasts, and misfortunes. It helps common development if the two partners are aware towards the alternate's desires. It likewise advances a conviction that all is good and trust that each is acting in accordance with some basic honesty.

Forgiveness puts the last seal on what happened that hurt you. You will in any case recollect what occurred, yet you will never again be bound by it. Having worked through the sentiments and realized what you have to do to fortify your limits or get your requirements met, you are better ready to deal with yourself later on. Forgiving the other individual is a superb method to respect yourself. It insists to the universe that you have the right to be upbeat.

While you ought to never stay in a relationship that risks your prosperity, all connections will require your sincere exertion and consistence with your partner's needs. Not abandoning somebody and attempting your absolute best to make it work are fair tasks to embrace. Utilize the above mentioned techniques to save your battling relationship and receive the rewards of an unbreakable cherishing bond.

<u>Best ways to deal with disagreements in marriage</u>

Each and every couple differs now and again. Impeccable similarity is unimaginable, yet sensibly working through imperfection can also work. The contrast between a cheerful couple and an unhappy couple is the manner by which they handle their contradictions.

The negligible actuality that your battle with your partner is anything but a sign there is a genuine inconvenience in your relationship. Actually, when taken care of appropriately, fighting can enhance your relationship. If you have never battle and never talk about your issues, you will never solve them. By managing clashes productively, you can pick up a superior understanding of your partner and find an answer that works for both of you. Then again, it is likewise workable for fights to heighten and make malevolence without settling anything. How might you enhance the chances of a successful resolution to the conflicts in your relationship? Hence, so as to develop and be fruitful in your relationship, you should use solid coping techniques for managing your disparities.

Never say never or always

When you're tending to an issue, you ought to abstain from making speculations about your partner. Proclamations like "You never assist around the house," or, "You're continually looking at your phone" are probably going to make your partner cautious. As opposed to provoking a dialog about how your partner could be progressively useful or mindful, this process is probably going to lead your partner to begin producing counterexamples of the considerable number of times they were, in fact, useful or mindful. Once more, you would prefer not to put your partner on the defensive.

Pick your fights wisely

If you need to have a valuable talk, you have to stick to one issue at any given moment. Troubled couples are probably going to drag different points into one exchange. When you need to take care of individual issues, this is most likely not the strategy you can take. Envision that you needed to consider how to consolidate progressively physical exercise into your day by day schedule. You would presumably not choose; this would likewise be an extraordinary time to consider how to spare more cash for retirement, sort out your storage room, and make sense of how to manage an awkward situation at work. You would endeavor to solve these issues each one in turn. This appears glaringly evident, however, without giving it much thought, a quarrel over one issue can transform into a complaint session, with the two partners exchanging fuss. The more grievances you raise, the more outlandish it is that any will really get completely talked about and settled.

Give early notification

No one reacts well to an assault, and regardless of whether it's not your aim, raising a touchy issue without early notification can feel like one to your life partner. A "notice" doesn't need to be not kidding or substantial – only a speedy notice of the point will do, enough to tell them you're endeavoring to figure out how to talk about it inside and out while regarding the way that they may require reality to get ready. A few people may be prepared to talk quickly, while others may request to visit the point in a couple of hours. Respect their demand.

Truly tune in to your partner

It tends to be exceptionally baffling to feel like your partner isn't focusing on you. When you interfere with your partner or accept that you recognize what they're considering, you're not allowing them to communicate. Regardless of whether you are certain that you know where your partner is originating from or realize what they will state, you could in any case not be right, and your partner will in any case feel like you're not tuning in.

At the point when your partner talks, rephrase what they say — that is, rethink it in your own words. This can avert misconceptions before they begin. You can likewise discernment check, by ensuring that you're deciphering your partner's responses accurately.

Pick the correct time

We all have certain times when our state of mind – and emotional energy– will in general be better than other people. You realize your companion better than anybody; approach them amid a period you know is great. Maintain a strategic distance from times when you realize they're exhausted and their enthusiastic limit with respect to the day has been depleted. It's far and away superior if you two can concede to an opportunity to handle the point, so it turns out to be more like a team effort.

Practice compassion

Practicing compassion will send the quick message to your partner that you're not hoping to do fight, yet rather endeavoring to work through your particular issue with both of your best advantages on a fundamental level. Lead the discussion by valuing their point of view or position. This won't just help you by giving you real compassion for your companion, yet it will assist them with feeling that they don't should be guarded.

Take an alternate point of view

Notwithstanding tuning in to your partner, you have to take their point of view and attempt to understand what standpoint they're maintaining. The individuals who can take their partner's viewpoint are less inclined to get angry amid a conflict talk.

Respect their independence

Now and again, in spite of their best attempts, two individuals don't come to an understanding. Particularly in a marriage, it very well may be difficult to accommodate the way that your life partner has such a different view; it can even make a few people question the authenticity of their association.

While marriage is an extraordinarily noteworthy relationship, the two individuals in it will dependably be self-ruling. Similarly, as you are qualified for your individual sentiments, so is your companion. And keeping in mind that there might be not kidding purposes of dispute that surface over and over, they should never be utilized to put down your companion.

By the day's end, marriage isn't tied to controlling your partner into like-mindedness. It is an unpredictable relationship that requires a gigantic measure of respect and open communication.

Find the ideal opportunity for a time-out

If you see yourself falling into negative examples and possibly find that you or your partner are not following the tips above, consider taking a period out of your conflict. Indeed, even a short break for a couple of full breaths can be sufficient to quiet hot tempers.

On Live-In Relationships In India

Live-in relationships in India are slowly seeing a growth in many urban parts of the country although it is still as tabooed as it used to be in the more rural counterparts of the country. However, just because live-in relationships are on the verge of an increase in India does not mean that the people here are actually very open minded towards the whole idea. There are definitely many troubles for a couple who is planning to get into a live-in relationship together. From legal problems to social ones, a couple really does have to have very strong belief in the system to work and great love for each other to enter such a set up. This is an overview on live-in relationships in the modern India.

The number of couples entering into live-in relationships is on an increase but their number of problems continues to be the same...

With the advent of technology and the Western influence on India that root more liberalistic perspectives, it is true that more couples are opening up to the idea of live-in relationships in India. This is especially true in the urban metropolitan cities like Delhi, Mumbai, Chennai, Bangalore and Hyderabad. However, this does not mean that the number of problems that these couples are likely to face is decreasing. The issues are still very persistent and the laws are not very straight about live-in relationships set up in India. Thus, if a couple does want to enter a live-in relationship, they must be prepared to fight many unconventional problems because at the root of it - such a choice in itself is a very unconventional thing to do.

Dealing with the families back home is never easy

Regardless of how open-minded one's family is, it is true that most parents cannot digest or accept the fact their son or daughter has made a choice to live in. For most part of it, they choose to stay in denial about the fact that their children are choosing a live-in relationship set up. Families primarily cringe at the very idea of live-in relationships because it makes them question the sanctity of the Union of a man and a woman.

It is an unacceptable arrangement for a man and woman to come together as opposed to marriage which is considered as a sacred bonding between the two. Another factor that leads to parents being very non accepting of live in relationships is that it is viewed as an abstinence from commitment and responsibility as opposed marriage where the couple commits to each other to live together and get through the thick and thin of the relationship, and to support each other and be there for each other in health and sickness!

Although the couples entering into live-in relationships might feel very serious and committed towards one another and do truly stick around for each other, it is hard for them to convince the families back home. Additionally, "What would the society think of you?" is a big question that parents throw at their children and unfortunately people who choose live-in relationships cannot give a positive counter answer to the same. So, if a couple is considering to choose to live in together, they have to make a trade off with their families being not very okay with it. The real scenario is that we will hardly find any families that openly embrace and accept such a setup.

Looking for accommodation is the next practical challenge

Even after a couple convinced their families about their decision of moving in and living in together successfully, that's not the end of troubles for the couple. In fact, the real troubles are just around the corner to barge right in. One of the biggest practical challenges here is to find a place to live in. With the traditional society set up, most landlords are very concerned with the question - *Are you single or a family?*

Live in relationship comes in between these because although the man and woman in the relationship is not single per se, they aren't a family either because they've not married each other. So, it becomes very challenging to actually dodge the question and communicate to the landlord about the nature of the couple's relationship. Most couples tend to lie to their landlords about the same and this is especially true when the couple is genuinely tired of trying to be honest and failing at convincing the landlords.

However, if and when the landlord does find out about the nature of such relationship, they might feel very furious and rage at the couple for lying to them. So, a couple needs to be look out for such insults and be prepared for the worst when it comes to house hunting. Strong couples who have good understanding and love between each other does get through these dark times somehow. The more important thing would be to not let such external influences affect the quality of the relationship.

Live-in relationships and the law

In the Western countries, there are strict laws that govern the nature of live-in relationships and provide a protection to women and men alike who are a part of such a set up. This is illustrated by the legal recognition of such relationships 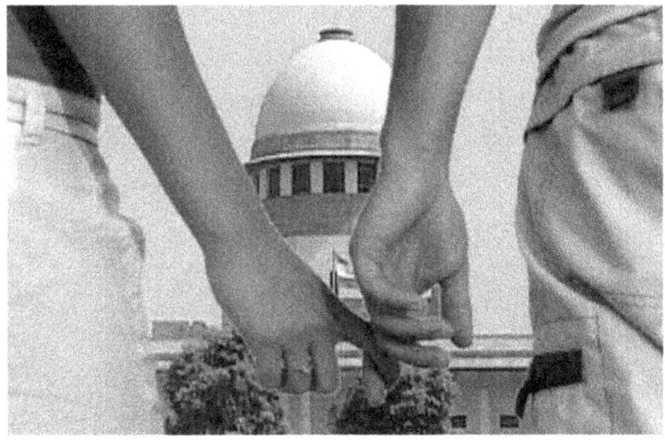 under the purview of the law by the Civil Union and Domestic Partnership laws and the laws of Cohabitation. In India, however there are no strong laws that deal with the set up of live-in relationships.

However, the Domestic Violence Act of 2005 in India has included live-in relationships under its purview where a man who is living in with a man as a couple is considered "a relationship in the nature of marriage" in the eyes of the law and the woman can go to the court if

abused. Thus, one can conclude that although there are no hard and strict rules that define the nature of live-in relationships in India, there are laws that are sufficient enough to cover and protect both the parties in the relationship when abused, and it's especially true for women.

Thus, a couple considering to live in must also consider that it might be a tough ride legally if and when things get ugly between the partners and one should enter such a set up only after having a fair understanding of the laws around it and with a belief that they'd not have to approach court, and if there does come a situation like that, the partners must be able to deal with it in a very mature and composed fashion without getting too worked up and frustrated or choose violent and abusive means of treating each other.

Final words

Above listed notes is a brief overview of what it is like to choose a live-in relationship set up in India. The reality however can be much more harsh than this and it really comes down to how strong both the partners in the relationship are. One should note here that as opposed to the popular belief that live-in relationships are devoid of work and are meant for people who wish to abstain from real responsibilities, they are actually a lot of work and can only be carried out when there's real dedication and commitment towards the relationship.

Having the willingness to go through all of these hurdles to be able to live-in together is very important and that's something that has to be decided by both the partners committing to such a relationship.